How to Sell What You Make

6 —

How to Sell What You Make

The Business of Marketing Crafts

Revised and Updated

Paul Gerhards

STACKPOLE
BOOKS

To Nanci,
for your patience and unwavering support

Copyright © 1996 by Paul Gerhards
Published by
Stackpole Books
5067 Ritter Road
Mechanicsburg, PA 17055

Printed in the United States of America

10 9 8 7 6 5 4 3 2

Cover design by Kathleen D. Peters

Library of Congress Cataloging-in-Publication Data

Gerhards, Paul.
    How to sell what you make: the business of marketing crafts /
Paul Gerhards.
        p. cm.
    Includes bibliographical references.
    ISBN 0-8117-2436-0
    1. Selling—Handicraft—Handbooks, manuals, etc. 2. Handicraft—
Marketing—Handbooks, manuals, etc. 3. Fairs—Handbooks, manuals, etc.
I. Title.
HF5439.H27G47 1996
745.5'068'8—dc20   95-37330
                                                             CIP

Contents

Crafts as a Business:
An Introduction

ARE YOU AMONG the many talented and creative people who dream of making a living off things crafted by your own hands? Are you one of those innovative people who design and make beautiful objects but sometimes wonder what to do with them once they are finished? You spent years studying your craft and now want more from your labor than just a way to pass the time. Chances are you are looking for ways to profit from the burgeoning crafts industry.

When you think of yourself as a craftsperson, what's the first thing that comes to mind? Most likely you see yourself as a creator of objects of utilitarian or aesthetic value, or both. Perhaps you consider yourself an artist or a holder of fundamental secrets to your craft that you have acquired through diligence and dedication. You did not just stumble into your job. You created it. Being a craftsperson is as much a matter of pride as is the work itself.

But have you considered that you are a manufacturer? If you consider being called a manufacturer abhorrent, put aside the associations the word has with factories and assembly lines, labor unions and strikes, department stores and shopping malls. "Manufacture" is just another word for "make."

It's not *that* you manufacture, it's *how* you do it. This doesn't necessarily mean that you do it all yourself and by hand with Old World tools; rather it refers to your connectedness with the design and the materials and the people you work with. This connectedness is fundamental to crafts and craftsmanship.

If you balk at the mention of "crafts industry," consider that crafts *is* an industry when viewed as a distinct group of productive and profitable enterprises. Crafts as an industry unto itself began during the 1960s with a resurgence in interest in handcrafted items. Makers of contemporary crafts came to appreciate the value of making things by hand, and consumers saw the value in owning things so produced. Craftsperson and crafts consumer joined hands and took both a symbolic and a real step away from the fruits of the Industrial Revolution toward something more personal.

Handicraft was every bit a facet of the back-to-the-land movement, which spawned a search for roots and a connectedness with things natural. Though many of the trappings of that lifestyle have gone the way of love beads and bell-bottom jeans, we are still in love with handicraft of all kinds. The catchphrase "high-tech versus high-touch" merely gives a new dimension to an older philosophy. Technology continues to solve problems (as well as create new ones) for an ever more complex society. But there is a sterility in technology, a coldness many of us can't get close to. Crafts, as well as all of the arts, is a way of keeping in touch with our humanity. For you, the craftsperson, this is, of course, good news.

For many craftspersons the first step in marketing crafts is the local crafts fair. Some fairs are held weekly, others annually, often in conjunction with regional celebrations. Crafts fairs are relatively easy to get into and offer a number of opportunities for both novice and veteran craftsworkers. The most important opportunity is in the sheer volume of people attracted to crafts fairs and markets. They are wonderful places to meet the buying public and fellow craftspersons and to learn what is selling this year and what isn't.

Selling directly to local shops and galleries is another way in which craftspersons market their wares. Just about every town or city has at least one crafts outlet, and taking the direct approach has many advantages over selling at fairs.

And there is yet another marketplace, one where people come for the sole purpose of buying, and buying in quantity: the national marketplace of the crafts trade show. Nearly every industry has at least one trade show each year, and the crafts industry is no exception. Crafts trade shows are where shop and gallery owners or representatives come to you to buy your crafts to stock their shelves.

The trade show is not necessarily a better way to sell crafts, nor are people who exhibit there better craftspersons. It is merely one of several marketing strategies available to enterprising craftspersons. But it is a sophisticated approach to selling crafts. It demands a high degree of professionalism.

The renaissance in crafts also has elevated the level of competition in the field. To get the sharpest competitive edge possible, many professional craftspersons no longer stack their goods on barn boards placed across sawhorses in an open meadow or parking lot, but in artistically designed booths on trade show floors. Competition here is keen. What's more, competition has infused the industry with ever-higher standards of professionalism. For the craftsperson this means learning a new set of ropes and gaining a thorough understanding of both the crafts business and general business principles.

This does not mean, however, that craftspersons who have chosen the trade circuit have forsaken their calling for pin-stripe suits and bottom lines. The very nature of crafts, as well as that of the people who make them with sincerity, seems to have kept in check, at least for now, the "let's do lunch" syndrome that has affected so many other industries. Crafts, in the broadest sense of the word, has always been a matter of culture first, business second.

When you last purchased something from a department store—an appliance, say—did you feel a connectedness with the worker on the line who turned nut *A* onto bolt *B*? Did you get a little piece of paper describing how the product was made and by whom? Probably not. Perhaps you have seen labels reading "Union Made in the U.S.A." Regardless of the national and class pride the phrase evokes, it's more a sociopolitical statement than a personal one. This is not meant to diminish the value of unions or an individual union member's pride in his work, whatever the job may be. But the larger the organizational structure, the less connection there is between the individual and the product. Things are manufactured not by people, but by companies that employ people.

Terms and Distinctions
The selling phrase in the crafts industry that has gained acceptance for its totally different connotation is "Handcrafted in America." This says an individual *created* the object. The piece has roots. It is the craftsperson's duty to the industry, then, to cultivate and protect that connection that keeps the roots strong and productive. As a manufacturer of crafts you have a wonderful opportunity to perpetuate a tradition, not only of craft and creativity, but also of personal and honest relationships in business.

Craftsmaking is a culture and a lifestyle. Craftsselling is a business. The successful craftsperson integrates both. Most small businesses fail due to lack of capital and poor management skills. To succeed in the crafts business the craftspersons must acquire more than just a dash of business acumen. Do not, however, confuse success with dollars. Define what success means to you, then strive for it. Though craftspersons rarely make a good hourly wage, they compensate by working more hours. The goal is earning a living, and all goals require sacrifice.

One such sacrifice is to shed the wardrobe and attitude of "starving artist" and replace them with those of a more entrepreneurial nature. This does not mean selling out to the system or replacing your apron with a three-piece gray flannel suit. What it does mean is learning what it takes to run a business and how to do it well. Creativity, and the pride it engenders, remains intact.

The crafts industry exists because it satisfies many of the wants and needs of consumers. Without demand there would be no crafts industry, at least on the scale it has achieved. The same holds true for an individual crafts business. It justifies its existence by satisfying the wants and needs of a portion of society through its products or services. A crafts business for its own sake ceases to be a business and becomes a hobby, fulfilling only the wants and needs of the craftsperson. One goal is no more or no less noble than the other, but understanding the difference between the two is essential for success.

Like any industry, the crafts industry has its own jargon. Words and phrases and concepts understood automatically by those involved sometimes sound confusing and ambiguous to the novice or casual observer of the trade. Some terms are interchangeable and others have specific meanings. Still others are cause for dispute among the players.

One of the most challenging areas to broach is that of crafts itself. Because crafts is such a diverse field, it is often difficult to draw, let alone recognize, boundaries between categories. It is important to understand that there are differences, because in some cases these differences impose limitations on which shows you can attend.

The word *craft* has broad applications. It can mean skill and dexterity in accomplishing certain tasks. In the crafts industry it is understood that merchandise is made largely by hand with skill and dexterity. A good carpenter has craft, but you would be hard-pressed to find a booth exhibiting new homes at a crafts trade show. But you will find furniture and all manner of other wood products.

It becomes tricky when some handcrafted items, items that for all intents and purposes are genuinely "crafts," are excluded from certain arenas. Take for example the woman who makes Christmas wreaths but was not selected to exhibit in a certain trade show. Why? Because wreathmaking was not considered a craft by the promoter. The promoter sets standards, guidelines, and limits, and what is considered crafts by one is not necessarily considered crafts by another.

Wreathmaking is better classified as what's called *country crafts* or *folk art*, and there are several shows where wreaths would be welcome. A country craft is no less a craft than, say, fine jewelrymaking, when undertaken with skill and dexterity, but the distinction should be obvious. It is absolutely necessary for the craftsperson to determine in which market her handiwork would be most accepted. Some country crafts may be appropriate at any show.

High-end and *low-end* are two concepts used to further distinguish crafts. High-end refers to crafts produced with the highest standards of quality and design. As such, they also demand the highest prices. Low-end describes those crafts at the opposite extreme. This is not to suggest that all low-end crafts are shoddily made and their design ill considered. High-end also refers to the relative uniqueness of the item as well as the degree of professionalism with which it's displayed. Even low-end crafts have high-end and low-end components. There is no one person who can make an objective, sweeping judgment of what is low-end and high-end. The judgment must be subjective. As a test, visit a crafts fair for the purpose of making such a judgment for yourself.

Fairs, trade shows, and *gift shows* are nebulous and sometimes overlapping terms. Crafts fair usually refers to a retail event, which is open to the public. Sometimes they are held in conjunction with local or regional celebrations, other times they are held within their own right. For the purposes of this book, any reference to *fair* means a retail event, with one exception. The American Craft Council holds several ACC Craft Fairs each year. These are major events and most have both trade days and public days.

Within the confines of this book a gift show is a trade show, but a trade show is not necessarily a gift show. A gift show caters to the gift trade and, therefore, has a focus far different from that of the crafts trade. Of course you might protest and say: "Just hold on one minute. Crafts can be gifts too, you know." Certainly they can. And that's why so many craftspersons exhibit at gift shows. In fact, some of the major gift shows have separate areas for crafts. As implied above, a craft item can be a gift, but a gift item may not be a craft. Also, many gifts are mass-produced abroad and are imported and distributed by large companies.

Many trade shows outside of the crafts trade welcome craftspersons. Exploring such avenues as fashion and accessories, architectural design, interior decorating, and office supply is encouraged. Each of these is a new frontier for craftspersons who have products filling a niche.

Retail outlets also have distinctions. A *gift shop* stocks its shelves with gifts much like any other store will stock its shelves with its specific kinds of merchandise. A *crafts gallery*, on the other hand, tends to exhibit crafts in groupings of work by individual craftspersons.

The *crafts mall* is a relatively new opportunity for some craftspersons. Typically, a crafts mall is a large store that is divided into small spaces that are rented or leased to craftspersons. The craftsperson does not have to be in attendance during business hours because mall owners or managers handle sales for him.

Show promoter and *show management* are synonymous. The promoter is the person or persons, under the auspices of a corporation, responsible for the show and all of its aspects from advertising the show to booking an arena. *Facilities management* is the governing body of the building or buildings where the trade show is held. The promoter deals with facilities management, but each exhibitor is responsible for following any established house rules.

The promoter's job is to bring craftspersons and buyers together for mutual benefit. Therefore the promoter must see to the wants and needs of both parties to ensure a successful show. One way this happens is that the promoter strives to make available for buyers a wide range of products and *price points*. There is nothing mysterious about price points, which simply is jargon for price.

One-of-a-kind, as the name implies, refers to individual craft items, each one unique. These pieces usually demand higher prices because of their uniqueness. (Indeed, any two items made entirely by hand are unique in varying degrees. When I refer to one-of-a-kind, I mean something that is unique in design and execution, something that cannot or will not be duplicated. I do not refer to, say, ceramic plates that due to the vagaries of the glazing process come from the kiln different from all the others, although by definition each is one-of-a-kind.) *Production crafts,* or *multiples*, refers to mass-produced items.

The terms *booth, display*, and *exhibit* are used interchangeably throughout the book as well as in trade show circles. Technically, though, they are different. The booth is the space you occupy in the show. Larger shows demarcate booth space with pipe and drape or another kind of partition. Smaller shows may not. Either way, you can construct a free-standing enclosure, a booth, as a setting in which you display your wares.

Your *display* is what you show, including your method of presentation. *Exhibit* takes display a step further. An exhibit generally shows and tells. For example, a series of photographs and text—or actual step-by-step models—depicting how you make your wares is an exhibit.

This book is not about how to get rich selling crafts. Its purpose, rather, is to do the following:

• provide an overview of how to sell crafts at fairs and directly to shops and galleries;

• introduce you, the enterprising craftsperson, to the crafts trade show;

• teach you how to apply to and prepare for shows;

• prepare you for what you can expect when you get there;

• demonstrate how you can apply generally accepted sales methods to the trade show; and

• give modest instruction on how to employ standard business practices to your crafts enterprise.

Whether you consider yourself a craftsperson, designer-craftsman, artisan, artist, or craftsmaker, if you can create fine-quality handcrafted items, you likely can sell them at a trade show. This book introduces you, the craftsperson with something to sell, to the national marketplace.

2

Crafts Fairs: Direct Link to Consumers

IN DAYS GONE BY, many craftspersons were nomads. Cobblers, coopers, tinkers, smiths, and others traveled the countryside plying their trades, exchanging goods and services for hard cash or a hearty meal. Most sizable towns had open-air markets where craftspersons and peddlers could hawk their wares. Today, craftspersons cling to their nomadic roots as they travel from town to town, crafts fair to crafts fair, selling what they have wrought. Neither the forum nor the purpose has changed much over the years.

Crafts fairs run the gamut of sizes from small-town events that serve as backdrops for celebration to expansive affairs in major cities. As with trade shows, retail fairs as a whole offer something for everyone. Unless your town has a permanent or semipermanent crafts marketplace, travel, and lots of it, is required to operate successfully on the crafts fair circuit.

Success on the retail circuit requires craftspersons to use many of the skills needed for success at trade shows (see chapters 6 and 7). Planning and organization are essential.

The more fairs you attend yearly, the more important scheduling becomes. Application deadlines must be met, booth fees or deposits paid, travel arrangements made. And it's ever so important to attend the right fairs. Research into fairs saves time and money by helping you avoid unproductive fairs or ones not suited to your business. How widely advertised is the fair? What is the expected attendance? Is it held outdoors, in a tent, or within a permanent building? What is the caliber of crafts exhibited? Is the fair held for its own sake or is it just one of many attractions of a larger event? How many exhibitors are expected? Is the fair open or juried? What is the fair's sales track record?

Salesmanship at the Retail Level

Good sales techniques can mean the difference between success and failure at any fair. The inexperienced exhibitor sits back and waits for potential buyers to express interest in buying. Craftspersons experienced in retailing don't hesitate to attract buyers in any number of subtle ways. There is no need for hard-sell tactics. A simple smile and a friendly greeting may cause a browser to buy from you rather than from a competitor. Talk about your products. Encourage fairgoers to handle your crafts. Explain how you make them, how they can be used. If you have something whose use can be demonstrated, do so regularly. That draws attention. Can you work on your crafts in your booth? This, too, attracts crowds. Pay close attention to those who stop by your booth more than once. Chances are they are trying to make a decision. Do what you can to encourage a decision in your favor.

Like other direct sales methods, retailing at crafts fairs involves meeting and greeting people. The more people you meet and greet, the more opportunities you have for sales.

One of the most important elements of your crafts fair business is your booth (see chapter 6). Your booth is your storefront. It must reflect you and your work in the most positive of manners. It must be rugged enough to withstand the rigors of the circuit and highly portable for easy transport and set-up. It must also, if necessary, be able to protect you and your work from the elements.

Advantages of Selling at Crafts Fairs

Crafts fairs are relatively easy to get into. Therefore, they offer a great opportunity to get your work before the public. This is an important step for any craftsperson. The crafts fair is one of the best mediums in which to test market new ideas and try out prices (see chapter 5). Trends often change as rapidly as the weather, and it's important to know what's popular and what isn't. The craftsperson with stale ideas and dime-a-dozen products won't do as well as the one with fresh and invigorating designs and products that speak for themselves.

Perhaps the biggest drawback to trade shows is their tendency to isolate craftspersons from the mainstream of consumerism. Craftspersons at trade shows deal with agents —wholesale buyers—rather than the buying public, the true creators of demand for crafts. The retail crafts fair serves as the link between you and crafts consumers. Talk with them. Find out what they like and dislike. Learning what the public wants and what it will buy—and providing it—is the margin between success and failure.

Disadvantages of Selling at Crafts Fairs

A big disadvantage to regularly selling at crafts fairs is the amount of time that must be spent on the road and away from your shop or studio. Nearly every weekend of the year must be devoted to travel, set-up, and selling. As a circuit-riding craftsperson, you will have to strike a constant balance between producing and marketing. The challenge is to have enough goods on hand to display and sell one weekend and still have time to replenish your stock.

Travel is hard work in itself, and not everyone is suited to the discipline it entails. If you have a family that accompanies you, especially one with young children, the regimen can be grueling for everyone.

Another drawback is in the nature of the fairs themselves. In many cases they are an adjunct to a greater event—a community celebration, for example. And even if they are independent affairs they possess a large degree of entertainment value. More people may come just for the fun of it than for the sole purpose of buying crafts. Still, no marketing expert will discount the importance of impulse buying.

How Crafts Fairs Differ from Trade Shows

A major distinction between shows that cater to the crafts trade and crafts fairs and other shows that cater to the general public is pricing. A trade show is a *wholesale* show, where you sell at a price much less than the consumer ultimately pays.

Craftspersons without adequate pricing experience find it difficult to cut their prices by half (the industry standard) to sell to trade buyers. Many novices to the crafts *business* do not recognize that they essentially are operating two businesses at the same time—a wholesale business and a retail business. The danger lies in treating these businesses as one, without realizing that each business has separate and distinct costs (see chapter 8). They arrive at their prices much as anyone else would: cost plus a little profit. Because their retail costs inadvertently are lumped together with wholesale costs, craftspersons selling at the retail level are likely to set prices somewhere between true wholesale and true retail. The consumer gets a bargain.

Unfortunately, retail merchants and craftspersons who wholesale exclusively are hurt by this practice because they can't adequately compete with prices set in such an arbitrary manner. The professional craftsperson who wholesales recognizes that, in theory as well as practice, retail prices aren't cut by half to sell to trade buyers; rather, wholesale prices are doubled to sell to consumers.

If craftspersons could sell directly to all of the potential retail buyers that could be reached via trade buyers (shop and gallery owners), there would be little use for trade shows.

Indeed, many professional craftspersons operate their own galleries or shops, and their prices reflect both wholesale and retail costs. But many of them rely also on the trade show to distribute their wares to a much wider consumer base. Essentially, those retail dollars that could be gained by selling directly to the public is the price they pay for distribution. But they are nondollars because, chances are, the craftsperson would not have reached those buyers in the first place. What's important is that wholesale prices be at a point that yields a comfortable profit and an acceptable standard of living for both wholesaler and retailer.

Since the price points you offer on an item can have an impact on the entire industry, strive to keep your retail prices competitive. If you have a wholesale account in the same area as a fair you attend, don't undercut the gallery's prices. Undercutting jeopardizes the account and puts you in competition with yourself. A better idea is to tell buyers where they can order more of your crafts locally.

Another big difference between selling at trade shows and selling at retail fairs is production scheduling. Because trade-show buyers place *orders* for products instead of buying existing stock outright, production schedules are based on orders written at the show or soon thereafter (with the exception that some inventory may be on hand to meet early delivery deadlines). Trade-show exhibitors take with them samples of their work to show prospective buyers. Retail circuit riders take with them a sizable portion of their inventory to sell to prospective buyers. Therefore, production schedules and output are based on upcoming events rather than past events.

The value of the retail fair should not be underestimated. Likely the crafts renaissance in the United States and Canada has as its foundation the retail crafts fair. Retailing at crafts fairs is the livelihood of numerous craftspersons all over the country. For many craftspersons these events are proving grounds and springboards to success in the trade world. Retail crafts fairs are the roots of well-established businesses.

3

The Gallery Connection

TRADE SHOWS AND RETAIL FAIRS are designed to bring buyers and sellers together in an atmosphere conducive to sales. This much is understood. At the crafts fair, once a sale is made, your relationship with the individual buyer is over, at least for the moment. It's true, word-of-mouth advertising could bring others to your booth. It's equally true some buyers will return for additional pieces of your work—if you are there at a later fair date, whether it's the next day, week, or year. But as a rule you deal one-on-one with the buying public and each sale is a one-time-only event. At the trade show you deal one-on-one with a representative of a bloc of consumers, and you are likely to establish an ongoing business relationship. This is the advantage of trade-show marketing; you have the ability to reach many through few.

Consider for a moment, however, the position of the wholesale buyer who owns or represents a gallery, gift shop, or other retail crafts outlet. In a broad sense he or she operates as you would at a crafts fair. Like the retail fair, shop owners make available to the general public a wide variety of crafts. It is the atmosphere that differs. Along with crafts for sale, the fair relies on its atmosphere of fun and entertainment to attract buyers for a short period of time. The shop relies on its atmosphere of a daily, ongoing representation of craftspersons and artists. For a fair to be successful for promoters, it must first attract a large and varied group of craftspersons and crafts. Here the difference between retail fairs and retail outlets becomes vague. In order for shops to attract buyers, they too must have a stable of reliable craftspersons to draw from.

Shop and gallery owners need craftspersons to represent and crafts to sell. It's how they make their living. Craftspersons who understand that shop owners need what they have—crafts—also understand that they offer a service by providing merchandise to dealers. Craftspersons who can provide a service are a commodity in themselves. It is up to you to offer the service and foster the relationship that follows.

How? By making your crafts and services available, by knocking on doors, by meeting and greeting the people who will sell your work to others. This said, the worst way to approach a shop owner is by knocking on the front door unannounced with a wagonload of goods in tow. The proprietor may be busy, unavailable, or have personal protocols that must be followed, and time and effort will be wasted on both sides of the sales counter. Once again, preparation, planning, and organization make the difference between amateur and professional behavior.

There is no one best way of approaching a shop or gallery. Some general guidelines may help, though. Always make an appointment with the person who has the authority to purchase your work. Dealing with seconds-in-command is of no value unless they have decision-making, contract-signing, and check-writing power.

Matters of Formality
The most formal way of approaching a gallery or shop is to prepare and mail an introductory packet. This consists of a

cover letter, résumé, sales literature, and slides or photographs of your work (see chapter 5). The purpose of the cover letter is twofold: to introduce you and to indicate a degree of professionalism. Type the cover letter on your business letterhead. Keep it short and to the point; it should never be more than one page long. Address it to the person with whom you eventually will do business, never "to whom it may concern." If you don't know whom it concerns, find out.

Explain in the cover letter that you are a craftsperson interested in placing your work in the prospective buyer's store and why. (The why is for the owner's benefit, not yours. See chapter 5.) Briefly list your qualifications, but save the details for the résumé. Tell the buyer you would like to make an appointment to further discuss doing business in, say, two weeks' time, and that you will be phoning soon to make the arrangements. Then list the other materials enclosed in the packet, for example, "For your consideration I've enclosed my résumé, photographs of my work, sales literature, and a wholesale price list." If you want any of the materials returned—photographs for example—say so near the end of the letter. Then make it easy for the buyer by enclosing a self-addressed, stamped envelope. As a matter of professional courtesy, this is a must. It also places the onus of response on the buyer. It opens the door for the buyer to send you a brief note of interest or lack thereof.

Make the résumé as brief but as complete as possible, one page at the most. It doesn't necessarily have to be the same kind of résumé you would use in applying for a job. Nor is it your life story. It should be simply an outline of your qualifications. List only those qualifications pertaining to your craft. That you have a degree in fine arts is one thing. That you have only a high school education but have served six years on the local school board and you coach a youth soccer team are things few others in the crafts business would be interested in. Be sure to list any awards received, affiliations with crafts organizations, trade shows attended, and how long you've been practicing your craft. Above all, avoid self-aggrandizement. The object is to sell yourself, but not by egotistic back-patting and puffery. Honesty and straightforwardness are of far greater value.

A week or so after you mail your packet, keep your promise and follow up with a phone call to arrange an appointment. Then bring along as many samples and sales aids as you think you need to influence a decision in your favor. Sales aids include appropriate display cases or racks and literature—anything that will make your crafts more attractive to the consumer.

Selling on Approval

Naturally, what you're after is setting up a wholesale account with a shop owner, just as you would at a trade show. If the owner declines to purchase your crafts outright, the next resort is to offer them on approval, a popular alternative to selling on consignment (discussed below).

The simplicity of the on-approval arrangement, as compared with the complexity of consignment, makes it attractive to the buyer. Selling on approval means you present the buyer a line of products and sales aids to display for a limited time, perhaps ten to thirty days but no more than sixty. At the end of that period the shop owner has two options: purchase the entire package at full wholesale value or return the merchandise, paying only for those pieces, if any, that were sold.

The financial risk for the buyer during this trial period is nil. And the risk to you is minimal. Your willingness to trust the gallery with your crafts indicates a high degree of sincerity and professionalism. What's more, if your crafts benefit the store in sales, there is no reason for the owner not to purchase the trial products and place orders for more under the standard wholesale arrangement. Shipping a few new products on approval along with regular shipments to an established account also is an excellent way to test the market.

The specific time period established in the agreement benefits both parties. For you it's an opportunity to test a market without tying up merchandise indefinitely. If sales don't occur it's a simple matter to determine why. Was the merchandise displayed prominently and marketed aggressively? If the answer is no, then chances are your products would not have received better treatment if they had been purchased outright; this was not an outlet useful to you. If the answer is yes, chances are the clientele was not a good match for your crafts.

For the gallery owner a specified time period is an opportunity to determine if his clientele is receptive to your crafts without indefinitely tying up valuable shelf space. If the match is not a good one, you part company, each learning a bit more about the market.

Regardless of the outcome, terms of the on-approval agreement must be spelled out in writing before the merchandise is placed to eliminate any cause for misunderstanding between the parties.

Selling on Consignment

Selling on consignment is a long-standing tradition in the crafts business. Though not entirely crafts specific, consignment selling is more prevalent in the crafts industry than in any other. Its advantages lean heavily in favor of the store owner, but even then they are often offset by an increase in paperwork. The advantages to the craftsperson are few, but they, too, have their offsetting factors.

In consignment selling the craftsperson places merchandise in the care of the store owner with no guarantee of sale. The craftsperson is the sole owner of the property until purchase by the consumer. The store owner has absolutely no monetary investment in the merchandise at any time.

Craftspersons find such an arrangement attractive for two reasons. First, because it precludes financial investment, it is often the only condition under which shop owners will take certain crafts, especially from unestablished craftspersons or those with extremely expensive one-of-a-kind pieces. Second, upon sale of an item, craftspersons realize a higher monetary return than they would selling at wholesale. Where the wholesale return is 50 percent of the retail price, standard consignment returns run from 60 to 70 percent. (But the trend is getting closer and closer to 50 percent, making it less attractive to the craftsperson and even more attractive to the retailer.)

In many cases, however, the extra percentage points are false profits. For example, if you sell ten pieces to the store at a wholesale price of $10 each, you take home $100 regardless of whether the pieces are later sold at retail. If you place the same ten pieces on consignment at 70 percent of retail you have a potential total return of $140. But suppose only five of the pieces sell and the remainder are returned damaged. Your financial return is but $70 on the five; the others represent a total wholesale loss of $50, leaving you with just $20 spread over the ten items. Clearly, selling on consignment is a gamble.

For the shop owner, taking crafts on consignment is an opportunity to stock shelves without investing financially in the stock. But the owner pays for that privilege in higher costs: 70 percent of the retail price goes to the craftsperson rather than 50 percent, meaning less profit if a sale is made. If a sale is not made, however, the absence of investment means no loss. Reversing the above example illustrates the point. A wholesale purchase of the ten pieces represents $100 in costs to the shop owner. If all ten pieces are sold at $20 each retail the owner realizes a gross return of $200, half of which pays the cost of purchase, leaving $100 in profit. (This, of course, is not all profit because as much as 95 percent of the $100 could go to cover operating costs.) If all ten pieces were sold on consignment, then the shop owner would receive in return just $60, or 30 percent of the combined retail price of $200. Just five pieces sold would net the retailer $30, but he would not have to absorb the $50 wholesale cost of the remaining five. Accepting crafts on consignment is safer than outright purchase, but that safety comes with a price.

An intangible cost to the shop owner who takes part in a consignment agreement is added paperwork. Once merchandise owned by the retailer is sold, it is money in the cash register. A consignment sale is something different altogether.

When a consigned item is sold to the public, the retailer then must buy it, as it were, from the craftsperson after the fact. This means that each sale must be recorded and followed up on with a check, either after the sale is made or on a regular basis.

Two prevailing reasons a shop owner will take crafts on consignment are lack of capital and little faith in the marketability of the crafts in question. What would you, the craftsperson, think of a business that was so low on capital that it couldn't purchase its stock? When you turn over crafts on consignment, essentially you are making an unsecured loan to the store with the hope of a high return. If lack of capital is indeed the problem, then it's a good guess that cash flow also is a problem. And this could spell problems for you. What if two or three of your pieces sell today, and the rent on the store is due tomorrow? The question is rhetorical because no one can know the mind of the person who has to pay the rent and the craftsperson but hasn't the money for both.

If the shop owner has little faith in the marketability of your work, then little or no effort will be made to sell it aggressively. You'd be better off looking for another outlet with better terms.

Expensive, high-end, one-of-a-kind items are the exception to the above examples that must be mentioned in defense of honorable retailers who handle such merchandise. Such items, by their very nature, aren't highly marketable and can certainly place a financial burden on the gallery owner. A large market exists for an earthenware teapot retailing at $40. But how many people would be interested in purchasing a working model of a Volkswagen engine made entirely of wood for $4,000? The gallery owner who pays a wholesale price for such a piece of handiwork stands a good chance of becoming a patron of the arts rather than a dealer of art.

Any consignment agreement should contain the following:
• description and quantity of each product;
• retail price and percentage to either consignee (retailer) or consignor (craftsperson);

• duration of consignment;

• method of payment (monthly or immediately upon sale); and

• onus of responsibility in case of loss or damage (inquire whether the store's insurance policy covers consigned items).

Crafts Malls

A recent trend in crafts retailing is the crafts mall. Individual craftspersons lease or rent display space within a larger store or group of stores. In most cases your work is juried before you are selected. Once granted a space, you are free to display your wares in any manner acceptable to the mall owner or manager.

Just as in consignment and on-approval selling, you are not required to attend your booth; the mall's personnel takes care of sales for you. But you are required to pay rent regardless of sales.

Before signing a lease agreement, ask other craftspersons about their success in the mall. You will want to know if the mall is in a high-traffic area and if the other craftspersons are able at least to cover their rent each month. You also will want to know of rent stability. Has it remained constant or has it been going progressively upward? Are there any hidden fees aside from rent?

Another important consideration is whether the owners carry theft and fire insurance.

The National Marketplace

WHEN YOU SELL CRAFTS at a retail fair, you bring your work into the local marketplace. Your customers are people who live in the area and may be attracted to the fair for a variety of reasons. The marketplace is diverse and defined only by its geographical area. You rely largely on the impulses of the fairgoers.

When you sell directly to shops and galleries, whether wholesale, on consignment, or on approval, you enter a more specific marketplace. Your dealers, or potential dealers, have defined that marketplace for you through their clientele. If these owners accept your work, chances are they have a good reason for doing so: They think it will sell and, therefore, will add to their income. But unless you have one or more sales representatives (see chapter 7), visiting all the potential outlets across the country would be an impossible chore. Even if it were possible, the costs would be prohibitive.

Imagine the time and money you would spend traveling the country in search of retail outlets for your crafts. Statistics indicate the average cost of visiting and setting up an account at an individual gallery is $150. The average cost of setting up a single account at a trade show is $50. Multiply the saving by the number of accounts you hope to set up and you see the value of entering an environment designed to attract buyers in large numbers from across the country. It is simply more cost-effective, both for you and the buyer. So the trade show can give you and your products valuable exposure to hundreds of serious buyers now and prospective buyers later on.

Tapping into the National Marketplace

What exactly is a trade show? To answer that question, let's look at an example from a completely unrelated industry: commercial fishing. Both coasts are home to thousands of commercial fishermen and cannery operators, and the industry is highly competitive. To compete, fishermen and fish handlers must have the latest and best equipment from radar to rowboats, nets to knee boots, power plants to canning equipment. So how do the fishermen know what's available in a burgeoning market? One way is by reading trade magazines, which are full of advertisements. Another is by attending trade shows where manufacturers bring and demonstrate the latest products. The trade show is like a living magazine, or catalog, where buyers—fishermen, fleet owners, and processors—can talk to sellers, see how things work, compare products and prices, even make deals.

A crafts trade show is not much different. The manufacturers are craftspersons just like you. They have invested time and money to be there for the sole purpose of showing buyers what's available on the market. And the buyers are the owners and operators of the thousands of gift shops and galleries and other retail outlets across North America. Hence the national marketplace. These buyers are not looking for just one item (although it's possible someone might be looking for that one-of-a-kind piece to serve as the centerpiece of his gallery), but all the items they need to stock their shelves for the upcoming season or for the entire year. And a portion of that stock they will buy from you.

But panic not! It isn't necessary for you to bring and show your entire inventory. The objective of the trade show is to show buyers what you make and how well you make it. If they like what they see and believe they can sell it, they will place orders. The buyers go away with the prospect of soon acquiring your quality crafts for their stores; you go away with the prospect of enough work to keep you busy, happy, and well fed for months to come.

So who, exactly, are crafts trade shows for, the maker or the buyer? The answer is both. There is a symbiotic relationship between the two, just as in any buying-selling relationship. The shop owner cannot exist without things to sell, nor can you, the craftsperson, exist (presuming a *desire* to exist on crafts) without people to buy your handiwork, and lots of it.

Marketplace Defined

Market is both a noun and a verb. As a verb it means to sell, or attempt to sell, products to customers. As a noun market, or marketplace, means a specific place where things are bought and sold: the meat market, the stock market, the supermarket. But *market* also is a concept, as in "what the market will bear." What the market will bear is based on the economic law of supply and demand. Is there a "market" for your crafts? In this sense, *market* is demand. Because there is a demand for crafts, there is a market for crafts. And it's a large market, a market composed of people who want what you have.

Competition at Trade Shows

The crafts business as a whole is so large and diversified that actual head-to-head competition between craftspersons is rare. Sometimes there is no personal competition at all. Consider the recording industry, the automobile industry, the food industry, or the appliance industry. Competitors here sell the same products, products easily exchanged one for another depending on personal tastes, styles, and loyalties. Because of the unique nature of crafts, however, each crafts business is an industry unto itself. The more conventional industries compete not only for a share of the market, but with one another as well. The competition facing the craftsperson leans more toward reaching a share of the market rather than competing head-to-head with another craftsperson selling exactly the same thing you do. It's more a question of whether you get your news from television, the newspaper, or a weekly news magazine instead of which station, newspaper, or magazine you subscribe to. The choice of media comes before the choice of medium.

The competitive atmosphere of crafts trade shows imposes high professional standards on craftspersons. These standards have both positive and negative effects on the industry. On the positive side they promote quality in craftsmanship and help satisfy a large-scale demand for quality crafts. The negative effects are more subtle. Many craftspersons fear that too much emphasis on competition and professionalism precludes innovation and stifles creativity. This is especially true when craftspersons become merely producers and sellers of the same things year after year just because certain crafts are profitable. Craftspersons who cease to be innovative for the sake of profit often find themselves suddenly standing still in a changing market.

You can overcome this complacency, however, by fostering diligence and a burning desire to force your creative and artistic abilities to the limit.

What Trade Shows Can Do for Your Business

Attending one or more trade shows each year can do a number of things for your business. Some are more obvious than others, but all are important. The trade show is a wide and varied network where veterans and novices alike can gain new insights on the industry and gather information about it. It's a place where you can get concentrated lessons on how to improve your marketing and selling skills. And it's a place where you can reap the financial rewards of hard work and dedication to your craft.

Welcome to the Network

The trade show puts you at the center of a network of people who work in your field and in the crafts community as a whole where you will learn more about the craft trade and market trends. Networking has become a common and valuable way of exchanging information. When you find yourself in a group of people who share common interests and goals, as well as common problems and frustrations, you also find a dynamism that cannot exist in isolation. Ideas and solutions not only are exchanged, they are created spontaneously when like-minded people interact. In crafts circles there is an openness and a camaraderie that is difficult to find in other industries. Craftspersons are willing and often eager to share their knowledge gained by experience.

Buyers, too, are a part of the network. Because buyers deal directly with consumers, consumers who live all over the country, they have a keen understanding of the market. They have a sense of where it is going and how it is traveling. Trade buyers are a valuable source of information about trends and about what may or may not work in the marketplace. Do you have an idea about a new product and wonder if the market is ready for it? Ask a buyer familiar with the craft. Is one of your products not moving as well as you'd like? Ask the opinion of people who are not buying. Crafts retailers are as much interested in the health of the industry as craftsmakers. It is their bread and butter too.

A third component in the network is the trade-show promoter. The promoter sets the stage for buyer and seller to meet and do business. As a secondary function, some promoters serves as educators. They publish newsletters and other literature filled with helpful advice on all phases of the business. Also available through show management are seminars and workshops addressing specific issues related to the trade. Promoters are motivated by the desire to enable buyer and seller to succeed, for without their success, the reputation of the show is compromised and attendance dwindles.

Trade shows can help you sharpen your marketing and selling skills. Marketing and selling are not synonymous, and understanding their difference is crucial to any business. Marketing has to do with customers, the people who buy crafts, the people who either like or don't like what you have (see chapter 5). Selling deals with products. To whom you sell— that is, your targeted market—is based on information gathered through the marketing process. There are any number of good books on marketing, the hows and wherefores of selling, but as always, experience is the best teacher.

Finally, a trade show can give your business the financial boost it needs. Millions of dollars' worth of orders are written at each major show. Though some crafts categories fare better than others, as do some individual crafts, the distribution of business is across the board. The craftsperson prepared to enter the world of crafts trade shows can expect to share in the rewards of the national marketplace.

Patience, Patience

Don't expect all this to happen during the first show. There is nothing wrong with great expectations, but any expectation has to be kept in perspective. All businesses take time to develop. The trade show is not a magic answer to marketing and selling; rather it's one of several stepping stones to success. Dozens of variables are involved. Some of them you have control over, others you don't. Perhaps the biggest obstacle is getting into the show or shows of your choice in the first place. In each show there is a limited number of booths, and there are hundreds of people who want one. You may not get into the first trade show you apply for, and, what's more, you may not get selected to exhibit in the same show the following year. But, just as there is a market for your crafts, so too is there a booth from which you can sell them.

Occasionally a new show is added to the schedule. Even if it's produced by an established promoter, it could get off to a slow start. Both buyers and craftspersons may be reluctant to invest in an unknown show. Studies show that it takes three years for a show to establish itself. Veteran craftspersons may wish to stick with the sure things. This leaves doors open for the novice.

Another factor to consider is determining which of the many shows held across the country is right for you and your products. Exhibiting at a show takes a significant investment of time and money. Aside from booth fees, which can be as much as $1,500, there are the other costs associated with exhibiting: travel and shipping, food and lodging, parking and recreation. Take care to select a show that attracts buyers interested in what you have. The character and atmosphere of each show is different, and you must be as scrupulous as possible in your selection. It's just another part of doing business. You wouldn't try to sell quilts in a pottery gallery or one-of-a-kind furniture in an airport gift shop. A first show takes an enormous amount of optimism to get through, but going in with little more than crossed fingers can be a costly mistake.

5

Getting Started

YOU ARE A SERIOUS CRAFTSPERSON with something to sell. You love your craft and desire to improve and perfect it. Perhaps you've tried to market your items door to door, so to speak, going from one gallery or shop to another in your area. You've left things here and there on consignment, and possibly you've sold some things outright. You've attended some local crafts fairs and have experience in dealing with the public. But for all of your effort, the income derived from your craft is merely a supplement to your "real" job. You have a terrific craving for independence. You want to be your own boss.

How Thick Is Your Skin?
Some self-employed people are better at business than others, but two things they all have in common are the desire to be independent and the tenacity and self-discipline to stick it out during the lean times. There's more to being in business for yourself than desire and tenacity. Personality plays a part. So does luck.

The marketplace for any item is volatile. What's popular this year might be passé next year. Suppose you catch the tail end of a popular wave and invest time and money developing a product to take advantage of it. For example, kaleidoscopes were a hot item in the 1980s. Although there is still some demand for them, their popularity isn't what it used to be. On the other hand you may develop something truly new and different, and you might find yourself on the crest of a wave. If you do you can be sure someone else is paddling hard right behind you. Or your new development might be a dud and sink like a rock.

Luck aside, you certainly need something else all successful businesspersons have in common: good management skills. The two biggest killers of young businesses are poor management skills and lack of capital. Of the two, for the craftsperson, lack of capital is of lesser concern. That's because you are in complete control of your growth. Craft is something that grows with the maker. No one wakes up one morning and says, "I think I want to be a craftsperson. I'm going right down to the bank and borrowing $100,000 to set up shop."

On the contrary, many crafts businesses begin either as hobbies or after years of formal study. Maybe you're an accountant who likes to make furniture at home. Or perhaps you have a degree in fine arts but support yourself as a commercial artist or a marketing consultant while making jewelry on the side. No matter how you start, the growth of your business is, and must be, under your control.

There is a paradox in the crafts business that you must come to terms with. To succeed in the trade-show world, you have to produce in volume. How much you produce is entirely up to you, and it doesn't matter if you produce one-of-a-kind items or multiples. You are the supplier, the key to the buyer's success. When you promise to deliver 1,000 mugs by June 1, you had better make good. Otherwise your reputation, not to mention your future business, suffers the consequences. A big complaint of wholesale crafts buyers is that craftspersons so often don't deliver as promised. There are two questions to answer.

• Do you want to produce in any kind of volume?

• Can you produce and deliver what you say you can?

This is not the place to go into the age-old debate of art for art's sake versus art for money's sake, or production work versus one-of-a-kind work. The choice is forever yours. A place for both schools of thought exists in the trade-show business. Many craftspersons apportion their time so that they can do both. The true artist pushes to the limits of his abilities, strives for the new and different, continually seeks to broaden his vision. It costs a great deal in time and money to develop and produce salable items of the quality that can demand appropriate compensation. To survive on one-of-a-kind work the craftsperson must have an extraordinary reputation, which in itself has its own price.

Pop Quiz

Rate yourself from one to five on the following questions, with five being the optimum rating.

• Can you maintain a high level of energy, making it easy for you to work continually without fatigue?

• Do you have the self-discipline to work long hours?

• Are you steadfast and not easily swayed or discouraged?

• Can you tighten your belt and make personal sacrifices for long-range goals?

• Are you resourceful and ingenious?

• Can you set goals and organize your thoughts and surroundings quickly?

• Can you make decisions quickly and accurately?

• Do you have a positive, friendly attitude?

• Are you honest and fair with yourself and others?

• Do you inspire confidence?

These are just some of the traits important to running a business. Scoring high does not necessarily mean you will make an excellent businessperson. Scoring low does not necessarily mean you won't.

Musical Interlude.   Once there was a young man who

longed to be a concert pianist. He studied and practiced, studied and practiced. One evening he went to a concert featuring a maestro he admired. Afterward he arranged a brief audition with the maestro.

"Do I have what it takes to be a concert pianist?" the young man asked. The maestro gravely considered the question for a moment then shook his head.

"Sadly, no," he said. "The best you can hope for is mediocrity."

The young man was crushed. He gave up the piano and went into engineering, where he developed a respectable reputation. Years later he had the occasion to again meet the once-admired maestro.

"Thank you so much for setting me straight," said the man. "Were it not for you I would be stuck in a mediocre career. Now I am a highly successful engineer."

"I remember you," the maestro said. "You had great talent. I was very impressed."

The man was stunned. "But you said the best I could hope for was mediocrity."

The maestro replied, "That's what I say to everyone who auditions for me. The ones who really have what it takes are those who shrug off the comment and go on to do great things."

Self-employed, Self-unemployed

Being self-employed means you work for yourself. And working for yourself can, and often does, mean being self-*un*employed. There are fast days and slow, fat months and lean. There is acceptance and there is rejection. Acceptance soon enough is taken for granted. Rejection too often is taken personally. It needn't be. Perhaps a gallery owner declined to carry your work. Perhaps a potential buyer at a retail fair told you that she could get a similar item three booths down at half the price. Or worse she told you that her twelve-year-old son could make it better. Rejection is part of the program. Shrug it off and persevere.

As your business grows, and you decide to step up to the trade-show circuit, there still is the chance of rejection. You may not be accepted into the biggest trade show in town on the first try or even the second. It happens. But there are dozens of local and national caliber to choose from. Some are more prestigious than others, and some *you* will have to reject. Keep trying. It's your business, and it's your business to make it grow. Consider the enterprising jewelrymaker who was not accepted to exhibit at a major show. She booked a suite of rooms in the hotel adjacent to the convention center where the show was being held, ordered a case of champagne, and set up her display in the rooms. She then went to the trade show and handed out invitations to jewelry buyers there. Buyers showed up at the appointed time, and the jewelrymaker did quite well for her investment.

Tenacity is the fuel that keeps your business going and growing. Large corporations, after a while, tend to become almost self-perpetuating. Not so with the small business. You must push your business in the direction you want it to go. Some days it might seem as though you're shoving a load of bricks across a desert. Other days it's a bobsled run down a mountainside and you find yourself screaming, "Whoa!"

These are the challenges facing the enterprising craftsperson. How in particular you face them depends upon who you are. Both the desert trudge and the icy slide take courage. By their very nature, craftspersons are creative and inventive. You didn't master your craft and develop your line overnight. So, too, it takes time and determination to develop your business into one you can consider successful on your own terms.

Examining Objectives and Setting Goals

Why do you want to attend a trade show? Chances are it's because you already have realized the importance of steering your business in the way you want it to go and grow. There isn't a self-help book that doesn't mention the value and importance of setting goals, both short- and long-term. This is good insofar as it gets you goal-oriented. (Most self-help books also are quick to add that you should reexamine your goals regularly and change them when necessary.) But, no matter how much you want to be a millionaire before you're thirty, you may have to lower your sights. You can do only so much business during a show. Success stories abound, however, as do stories of the other sort. It's helpful to set sales goals, if for no other reason than to test your mettle.

The Intangible Benefits of the Trade Show

Recognize that sales are not the only objective. Attending a trade show offers a variety of intangible benefits, especially after you've been to one or two. The biggest is the volume of buyers who attend. Where else can you talk in person to a gift-shop owner from Seattle and a gallery owner from Fort Lauderdale at practically the same time? Where else can you meet hundreds of prospective buyers? You reap profits by establishing and maintaining an image not only of a personal nature, but also of goodwill and understanding.

Establishing new relationships is just as important in the long run as filling your production schedule. For example, suppose a buyer has come to the show with a specific budget. He knows what he wants and has completed his shopping for the trip. He comes by your booth and likes what he sees. You develop a business relationship potentially lasting for years. Or suppose this same buyer isn't interested in your wares but knows someone for whose store your line would be perfect and makes the introduction. The "what ifs" are endless. Call it being in the right place at the right time. Call it dumb luck. Regardless of what you call it, the wider your exposure the greater your chances of expanding.

The trade show also is the perfect setting for acquiring new information and testing new ideas. If you've come up with a new product, show it along with your regular items. You'll know quickly enough if it generates interest. Trade buyers know their clientele. If a buyer sees something new and novel and knows he can sell it in his store, he'll likely buy it from you. On the other hand, he might be attracted to it personally but may not be convinced of its marketability. Even the best ideas can bomb, and you want to know about it before you go into production. Have you ever seen a prospective buyer stop by a booth, pick up an item, and say something like, "This is simply wonderful," then put it down and walk off? At a retail fair, that single buyer is representing himself, but at a trade he might represent an entire market.

You can discover trends at a trade show. Talk to buyers to find out what their regular clients are interested in. Retailers stay in touch with market trends because it helps them stay in business. You, too, can take advantage of the information. How long the trend (or trendiness) will last is anybody's guess, but the trade-show floor is where you'll likely find out that interest is beginning to wane. The trade-show floor, however, is not the place to go mining for ideas to copy outright. Ethical considerations and your reputation aside, many ideas and designs are copyrighted.

Crafts trade shows offer a camaraderie not often found in other industries. A show offers an opportunity to network with others in your field. A good example of the value of networking is checking references of buyers (a topic covered in more detail in chapter 6). If a buyer places a $500 order with you, it's a very good idea to make an effort to learn if the buyer is dependable.

Do not expect instant monetary success from your first trade show. Trade shows offer more than one opportunity for craftspersons, and sometimes it takes years to appreciate the dollar value of what at first seems an unlikely contact or a fruitless expedition.

A Goal Is a Goal Is a Goal
When setting goals and objectives for a show, consider them as tiny facets of a larger goal, say, earning a living from your craft. Begin by writing down what you hope to achieve and express it in a complete sentence. This turns a thought or idea into something concrete. Once on paper, ideas become realities that must be acted upon or rejected. Start with the largest

goal and break it down into smaller segments. The smaller the segments, the more manageable they become. Notice that the short-range goals are steps along one or more paths to achieving longer-range ones. Eventually your main goal will be broken down into a large number of small, easily handled tasks (goals in themselves). When possible, each goal should have a time limit. Next, follow the plan methodically, discarding those steps that no longer apply and adding others as needed.

Be reasonable about your goals; don't confuse them with desires. You need at least to have a reasonable chance at succeeding and to be realistic about those chances. Setting goals can be a tricky business, especially if success in reaching those goals hinges on factors that are out of your control. For example, you may write, "I will attend the ACC Craft Fair in Baltimore next year." You list and follow all of the steps for application. If you are accepted, you then list and follow all of the steps to get to the show. But what if you are not accepted? Once you send in your application, you have no control over the selection process. A more realistic goal, until you are an established exhibitor at one or more shows, is: "I will apply to six shows for the following year." Your goal is to apply, something that is in your complete control.

Realistic sales goals are a slightly different matter, but you still have some control over them. The key word is *realistic*. Say you are planning for your first show and set a goal of writing orders totaling 1,000 pieces. This may be unrealistic because, first, you don't know the buyers' minds. Suppose you made sales to every buyer present in your field but for only 750 pieces? Second, you can't force people to buy. So you might modify your sales goal to read, "I will make personal contact with fifty buyers." This is not only realistic but attainable. Through your research on a particular show, you already know who the buyers are, and you've sent these buyers a pre-show promotion to familiarize them with you and your wares. Again, once you're established it's easier to set figures.

Production goals also are under your control. If you find that for the next six months you have more work than you can handle by yourself, just list the steps it takes to increase production. It may require streamlining your operation and even hiring employees.

In setting goals also consider alternative ways of achieving them. Few destinations have only one road leading to them, and few goals have only one course of action necessary for their achievement.

Selecting a Trade Show

The major crafts trade shows across the country and throughout the year range from high-end production and one-of-a-kind crafts shows to gift shows to country- and folk-art shows, all of which attract thousands of buyers. Dozens of smaller, locally produced crafts shows fill market niches of their own. And there are myriad shows not exclusive to the crafts world, but nonetheless fertile ground for an enterprising craftsperson.

It's not only impossible to attend all these shows for financial reasons, it's also not wise for professional reasons. Exhibiting in the wrong show can be as detrimental to your business as exhibiting in the right show can be a boon. This book does not presume to tell you which shows are right and which are not. The choice is entirely yours.

Many show promoters send prospectuses to potential exhibitors. Request one and read it. The first and most important factor in selecting a show is the audience. What kind of buyers, and how many of them, does the show attract? The underlying question is in what kinds of shops, stores, or galleries you want your wares to be sold. Buyers come from all over, and it's to your best interest to know where they come from.

One way to find out is to work backward. Spend some time visiting a wide selection of outlets. Ask the owners which shows they attend and why. While you're at it, you can always make your pitch and set up new accounts. (A prerequisite for acceptance to some shows is that you already maintain or have maintained a wholesale account.) Talk to owners of those shops where you would not consider selling your crafts. This information gives you an idea of what shows to stay away from.

Ask other craftspersons which shows they attend and why. Understand, however, that established craftspersons tend to stick with shows that are successful for them. Sometimes the reasons for their success are not so easy to pin down, and show loyalty plays an important role.

How Much Does It Cost?

The cost of attending a trade show is more than just the booth fee. It pays to find out early what other costs are involved. When you apply to a show, usually a booth deposit must accompany the application. How much is it and when is the balance due? If you have to cancel, how much of the fee will be refunded? Do you have to pay extra for drapes, tables and chairs, or electricity, or are these costs included in the booth fee? What about the cost of hiring union labor to unload and set up your booth? Does the promoter prepay wages of union laborers? Does the trade show you wish to attend require that you be a dues-paying member of the sponsoring organization? (Don't discount the benefits of membership beyond trade-show participation. They might be just what you need.) What about shipping, travel, and accommodations costs?

What does the show promoter provide? Some provide poles and drapes, for example, to separate one booth space from the next. Some spaces merely are marked on the floor. How you design your booth depends on this, as well as the booth size. A high booth fee may seem exorbitant at first, but it may include amenities you otherwise would have to pay for out-of-pocket.

The trade-show environment is geared to bring buyers and sellers together. Show management strives to make the atmosphere as conducive as possible for the success of both ventures. Generally, how you sell is up to you. But as with most things there are restrictions, and you should know about them in advance. Do you have to show your own work, or can you send a representative? Can you serve snacks in your booth? Is there a limit to the number of personnel you can have in your booth at one time? Can you share your booth with another craftsperson or sublease a portion? Can you play music or show a video tape to attract buyers?

The location of the show is probably one of the easiest things to make a decision on, but knowing what city the show will be in isn't enough. Will the show be held in a convention center, sports arena, or hotel? Downtown or in the suburbs? Are hotels close by, or will you have to commute? If you drive to the show in a camper or RV, will you be able to stay overnight in the parking lot, or will you have to drive to an RV park?

Timing is another consideration. Trade-show promotion is a business in its own right. Cities compete with one another by building convention centers to attract large groups of people who will spend money on the local economy. Trade-show promoters take advantage of these large facilities to attract as many craftspersons and buyers as possible. Lots of craftspersons mean lots of buyers, lots of buyers mean lots of craftspersons.

Trade-show promoters also compete for exhibitors and buyers. Some shows are scheduled to coincide, and show promoters often cooperate by providing shuttle service between sites. For you, the exhibiting craftsperson, this can be good or bad. On the negative side, a competing show can draw buyers away from your booth. On the positive side, the competing show might attract buyers who will visit your show and your booth because it is convenient. Buyers take advantage of the situation merely because more can be done in one trip, provided the buyer is interested in what each show has to offer. The same can be considered true for the craftsperson. If competing shows run simultaneously, consecutively, or overlap by a day or two, it may be possible—with help and good planning—to exhibit at both.

When to Start
The selection process can be arduous and time-consuming. It's an investment in your business and should not be taken lightly. The best time to begin zeroing in on your first show is

a year and a month before the show you hope to attend. This gives you plenty of time to meet show deadlines and to prepare and take advantage of preshow promotions. The extra month is to allow you to arrange to attend the show as a guest before you attend as an exhibitor. True, this is an added expense, but if you discover the show is not for you, you save in the long run. You can see for yourself what kinds of wares are exhibited and who the buyers are. You can ask questions of exhibitors and of show management.

Although trade shows are not open to the public (with the exception of those that offer both trade and retail days), as a craftsperson you likely will be able to acquire a guest pass to the show. Simply call or write the promoter and explain that you wish to visit the show before you apply to exhibit and ask for a guest pass. Some established exhibitors frown upon this practice, fearing that visiting craftspersons will steal ideas from the paying customers. Promoters, however, understand this is a legitimate way for potential exhibitors to fully evaluate their show.

If you know a fellow craftsperson who plans to attend a certain show, ask if you can go along as a booth worker. Being an assistant is an excellent way to learn the ropes before heading out to sea on your own.

Once you have selected a show or shows in which you want to exhibit, write or call and ask for an application. Application procedures vary with each promoter; what follows is only a general description of the process unless otherwise noted. With your application, be prepared to submit a booth deposit of as much as $375 (refundable if you are not selected), five color slides of the merchandise you will be exhibiting, and possibly a screening or jury fee. In some cases you can submit color photographs or actual samples of your work.

The application package also details when the remainder of the booth fee is due, other deadlines, and other important information. Follow the instructions carefully. If you are late with your balance, you may be penalized with a late fee or, worse, canceled from the show altogether.

The Verdict Is In

Show organizers receive thousands of applications for each show they hold. There are always more applicants than space available. It's a fact of life that some applicants will be turned away. How do promoters decide who will get in and who won't? In a word: jury. The jurors judge your work on its merit and how it fits into the show's established criteria. Some shows have a seated jury of craftspersons and other professionals in the industry who use a point system to select exhibitors. Other promoters use a more relaxed approach, an internal committee perhaps, which considers not only the quality of the work itself, but the applicant's professional standing in the crafts community. Nevertheless, standards are usually high, and your best chance is to strive to meet them.

The jury system has its drawbacks, however. Jurors are people just like you. They have their own biases and standards, no matter how objective they try to be. Imagine if you were charged with selecting 500 exhibitors out of 1,000 applicants. How would you do it? You would have to draw the line somewhere (no fair leasing more space to accommodate 500 more booths). Eventually, you may even find yourself becoming (gasp!) arbitrary. Sometimes jurors are arbitrary, too. Or maybe their eyes are blurry from looking at thousands of slides, or maybe they're grouchy on the day they look at yours.

In most cases, a jury need not tell the rejected applicant the reasons for its decision. As the rejectee, you are left in the dark. "What did I do wrong?" you ask. You may never know. Perhaps you did nothing wrong at all. It's another instance where luck plays a big role.

Another thing newcomers should be aware of is the seniority system. Those who exhibited last year have a chance to do so this year, provided they meet the application deadlines, of course. Exhibitors are assigned seniority points for each successive year they exhibit, which apply to the following year's show. Some shows offer multiyear contracts under which further screenings are not necessary, provided there is no change in products. Some promoters offer sabbaticals to tenured exhibitors. For a small fee you can opt to stay away from the show or shows for a year without losing seniority.

"So, how do I get in?" you ask. "It's the old-boy network after all!" It's true newcomers have a harder time than the established craftsperson in getting into a show. But that's what competition is all about. There are spaces available for newcomers. If you are not accepted, ask to be placed on a waiting list.

The Criteria

Trade-show promoters are scrupulous when selecting exhibitors. They want to know exactly what you plan to exhibit. Your work will be selected on quality, design, originality, function, and countless subjective criteria. In addition, show management wants to know what portion of your work is production, custom, and one-of-a-kind. What you submit on film must be representative of what you will be exhibiting. The American Craft Council, for example, requires that your slide submission be in direct proportion to your exhibit: If you submit three slides of production pieces and two of one-of-a-kind work, then three-fifths of your exhibit must be production work and two-fifths one-of-a-kind. Also, if you submit slides of, say, turquoise and wood belt buckles, tie clips, and money clips, don't show up with a line of desk accessories, too. You will be asked to remove the desk accessories, no matter how good they are.

When a jury or other panel selects exhibitors, it often uses criteria not directly associated with the work itself. The Rosen Group, for example, first considers the applicant's experience and seeks referrals from other exhibitors and from buyers. The quality of slides and literature indicates a level of professionalism, also important to the selection process. To attract the widest range of buyers, the agency considers products by virtue of their quality, design, uniqueness, and price points.

The American Craft Council has developed a jury system that has been adopted by some other exhibiting organizations. Each craftsperson is required to send five 35mm slides of the work to be exhibited. These slides are loaded into five projector carousels so that all can be seen simultaneously by a jury of craftspersons, gallery owners, and other crafts professionals. The projected images are identified only by number to eliminate bias. Each jury member assigns the grouping with a value: one, two, four, or five. No threes are permitted, thus eliminating indecisiveness and middle-of-the-road judging.

Slide Work

The importance of submitting quality slides cannot be overstressed. Photography, not to mention crafts photography, is an art in itself. If you know the rudiments, by all means shoot the work yourself. But don't submit the slides if they are not excellent. Fuzzy, out-of-focus, or poorly lighted and ill-defined shots will not fare well with the jury. The alternative is to employ the services of a professional photographer. Many people with cameras call themselves photographers, but there are degrees of craftsmanship. Also, a photographer who takes excellent outdoor shots for newspapers and magazines may not have the expertise and equipment for studio shots, which make the best slides for judging. Examine the photographer's portfolio to make sure he can do the job.

When discussing your needs with a photographer, make sure you explain exactly what you expect from the finished product. If necessary, show him or her similar pictures from trade magazines or drawings of how you want your pieces to appear. The less information you provide, the more artistic license the photographer will take.

When projected on-screen, many craft items—jewelry for example—appear much larger than life. Often these shots give no reference to actual size. Suppose you have a delicate porcelain cup two inches tall. Will the juror see it as it really is, or mistake it for a piece of crockery large enough to bathe in? Make sure your work is photographed in such a way as to prevent ambiguity.

When sending slides, unless otherwise instructed by the promoter, mail them in a plastic holder, the pocket kind that fits into a binder. Never send them loose in an envelope. Mark each one with your name and address.

Another good reason for using only slides of the best quality is that, if your work is selected, the promoter may want to use one of your slides for promotional literature. You also can use these shots for your own promotional literature as well as for advertising in trade journals, so make sure you have plenty of copies of the best slides.

Advertising and Publicity

Once you've been accepted to exhibit at a show, you have more work to do. Aside from getting your exhibit ready and making travel and shipping arrangements, you have to get the word out. Marketing experts estimate 85 percent of any successful sale takes place *before* you talk to a customer, by way of advertising and publicity. No business can operate within a vacuum. If people don't know what you have to offer, there is no reason for them to come knocking at your door—or your booth. Let's look at what advertising and publicity can do for you.

To be most effective, advertising should be ongoing, a constant reminder you are in business. Suppose you are leafing through the newspaper one day and see a catchy ad for a plumber. You don't need a plumber, so you don't pay the ad further attention and soon forget all about it. But next month, on a Sunday evening, your water heater springs a leak. You grab the Yellow Pages, hoping to find a plumber who can come immediately. Suddenly you see an ad for the plumber you saw advertised in the paper. Chances are you'll call him first, for no other reason than name recognition. The plumber gains your business because he made a psychological introduction of himself through his ads.

The psychological power of advertising is enormous. A one-time, small, ill-conceived ad suggests that the advertiser is operating on a shoestring (which might be true). This detracts from the *apparent value* of the product, that is, the value *you* subjectively apply to the product. Large snappy ads, especially those that appear regularly, suggest that the adver-

tiser is serious about his business, can afford to "do it right"—
and the product has greater apparent value.

Advertising and publicity go hand in hand, and the results
are much the same. But there is a difference. Advertising is
paid for. As long as the ad is in good taste, any medium will
happily exchange their space for your dollars. Publicity is free
or costs little, unless you enlist the services of a public rela-
tions firm. Once you've paid the price, advertising is auto-
matic. Getting publicity, especially in the media, is not
guaranteed. Because it is essentially free advertising, it is the
decision of the media whether to grant you access. This decision is based on what it can do for them, not what it can do
for you, though the media is well aware of how you benefit.

Who, What, When, Where, Why, and How

The basic factors in advertising and publicity, the five *W*s and
an *H,* are who, what, when, where, why, and how. These are
essential, though the *why* and the *how* are often implicit
rather than explicit. No ad should be without them. The exception comes when a product or service is so well known that
one factor implies the others.

When two people meet for the first time, the first bit of
information that passes between them is *who* they are; names
are exchanged. As an advertiser, this is the first bit of information you want to convey. Buyers, whether retail or wholesale,
want to know who they are dealing with. In many retail transactions, however, the *who* is often overlooked. People see
what they like and buy it. The further removed you are from
your product, the further removed you are from the buyer. It is
up to you to make yourself known. Advertising is how you
establish name familiarity. Who wants to be known as "You
know, that woman who makes those lovely wall hangings"?

The *what* factor is the essence of the message you wish to
convey. Perhaps it is your handmade paper. But it could be
more general, such as an exclusive showing of your work at a
local gallery. In any case it is the cornerstone of your ad or
publicity campaign. The best conveyance of *what* is the illus-
tration; ads are best when they are visual. Even on radio, the

best ads are those that paint mental pictures, taking advantage of the power of imagery to get the message across.

If you are celebrating the grand opening of your gallery, the *when* tells the date and time. If your craft is the focus, the *when* tells availability—hours of business for example. The same holds for the trade show. *Where* takes its cue from what and when.

Why is often the most difficult message to convey, perhaps because it deals more with the psychological and emotional sides of advertising. *Why* concerns itself with the target market's wants and needs. If the overt message of the ad is to "Celebrate the grand opening of Eye of the Beholder Gallery," the covert message must somehow explain why anyone would want to attend: "Come see the latest in American crafts designed to meet your decorative needs."

How can be as simple as dialing the phone: "Call 555-1960 for a free catalog." Or it can mean traveling 1,000 miles to the trade show in which you will be exhibiting: "Please drop by and see me at Booth 392 at the Boston Buyers Market."

Preshow Promotion

One of the most valuable tools available to the trade-show exhibitor is preshow promotion. This is a mailing sent to buyers who will or might attend the show. Check with the promoter to see if a mailing list is available or ask if the promoter can do the mailing for you. If not, compile your own list. Ask the promoter about sources. Other sources for names are telephone directories (a good library has directories from across the country), business guides, local and national crafts guilds and organizations, and the American Craft Retailers Association. An alternative is purchasing a mailing list from a company specializing in the field. Check the Yellow Pages of your phone directory for listmakers.

Attending trade shows is routine for buyers. They attend whether you do or not. So why a preshow promotion? Buyers, like all people, like and need acknowledgment. The preshow promotion is a personal invitation from you not only to attend

the show, but to also stop by your booth. If the buyer doesn't
know you and is not familiar with your work, the promotion
serves as an introduction. With regular customers, the preshow
promotion gives you a perfect opportunity to show them
what's new in your line. If there are changes in your line, or
you have new products, don't wait until just before the show
to let your regular buyers know about them. Once you've
established a mailing list, make it work for you. Your promotion package includes sales literature, price list, and order
form. If you have regular customers, include a personal note.
Don't forget to include your booth number.

As a service to exhibitors, many show managers provide
craftspersons with promotional materials for a particular
show—postcards and such—for the express purpose of mailing
to buyers in advance of a show. By all means take advantage
of what's available.

The Press Release: Free Publicity
The press release provides the public with news, information,
and entertainment. As formidable as it sounds, the press
release is nothing more than a short piece that informs the
media—print or broadcast—that a newsworthy event is about
to take place. What is newsworthy is always up to the discretion of the editor who will eventually publish (or toss) your
release. It is imperative, therefore, that your release be
pegged on an event.

What is newsworthy? That depends. If you live in a small
town in South Dakota, and you are going to a trade show in
Boston, the editor of the local paper might consider a press
release about your trip. Don't bother sending one to the *Boston
Globe*. But if you are the designer of something new, different,
and trend-setting on a national scale, someone at the *Globe*
might be interested. Have evidence to back up your claims.
What's big news in a small town is more often than not an
annoying fly to a big-city editor.

Check your local paper for examples of what is newsworthy. There you will find dozens of short pieces announcing this
meeting or that award given or the odd appointment made.

Chances are the news arrived at the paper in the form of a release. Are you opening a gallery or showing at one? Are you introducing a new line of crafts or giving a lecture? Did you receive an award for high sales or other honor at a recent show?

To get an idea of who might be interested, obtain a copy of your regional media guide. This is a directory of all print and broadcast media in your region or state. Check for it at the library, chamber of commerce, or other agency. It tells you names, addresses, and phone numbers of people to contact.

Your news release must look professional. Write in on your business letterhead. The *copy* (material to be set in type for printing or to broadcast) should be typed double spaced for easy editing. At the top type "For Immediate Release" so that there is no question of intent. Then type "Contact:" followed by your name and telephone number. Next comes a headline that sums up the message to follow. Then write the lead. All five *W*s and the *H* should be as close to the top of the lead as possible, though not necessarily in the first sentence. Determine which of the six elements is most important and begin with that. Follow the lead with less important but relevant background material and a quote or two. Stick to the facts. Never add self-aggrandizing adjectives or statements. The editor is not interested in your ego, only your news.

Writing a press release longer than about two pages is a waste of time. Even if you think your information is so important or so interesting that the story merits 1,000 words, the editor probably won't agree. If the release runs more than one page, type "More" at the bottom of each page. Type "End," "-30-," or "#" at the end of the piece.

A photograph always is a good companion to a story. Newspapers use eight-by-ten-inch or five-by-seven-inch glossy black-and-white photos. They can make black-and-white pictures from color prints and slides, but the effort and cost involved is not worth the bother. Magazines make more use of color slides, but they must be of the highest quality. The high cost of producing color pictures precludes their use for press-release material. Never send product shots unless accompanied by a good photo of you, preferably one of you doing something. Newspapers are people oriented. They like photos of people, not things. Put your name and address on the back of each photo. Do not use pen or pencil; use a sticker, taped label, or grease pencil. Avoid using a rubber stamp directly on resin-coated photo paper. The ink can smear and even transfer to the face of other prints. Identify the people in the photo and describe the activity on a separate sheet of paper, which you can tape to the back of the photo. Never fold a photograph; it's useless if you do. If you want the photo returned, say so, and include a self-addressed stamped envelope.

The press or media kit is an extension of the press release. It appears in folder form with more information. It includes brochures, photographs, a business card, a press release, and background information. It may also include copies of other stories published about you and your work.

Whether you send a press kit or a release, be aware of deadlines. Daily newspapers have the shortest lead time. A deadline for a weekly is usually a week before the edition in which you want your story or ad to appear. Magazines are something else altogether. Plan on a lead time of three to six months. In any event, check it out with a phone call. It's also wise to send your material to the right editor. Again, a phone call will do the trick.

Do not be surprised if your carefully worded press release is rewritten from top to bottom and material left out. There are three reasons this might happen, especially if the paper in which it appears is larger than a small-town weekly. First, in your ardor you missed your own point. It happens all the time. What you think is the most salient point may not really be so; editors are trained to recognize such things. Second, the editor or writer will force your copy to conform with the paper's style. Third, editors know that press releases go to many different places. They don't want their stories to appear word for word in other papers.

Your main concerns with press releases are accuracy and clarity. A fuzzy release produces fuzzy results. If the editor or writer can't follow it, neither will readers.

Sometimes a press release sparks an editor's or reporter's interest. If that happens you may find yourself the topic of a feature story—complete with interview and photography session. This kind of publicity is invaluable. Frame it and display it in your booth. Send a copy to your valued customers. And don't forget to ask the photographer if he can make extra prints for you or if he will give you the negatives. It may cost you, but you'll never get that chance again.

Free-lance Writers: More Free Publicity

A story in a local paper also can lead to bigger and better publicity. Consider it gravy if it happens to you. Free-lance writers always are on the prowl for good stories. One place they look is the newspaper. (Craft fairs also are good stomping grounds for specialty writers.)

With a free-lance writer, however, you have even less control over the content of the story than you do with a release-generated story (the same holds true with a staff-written news feature). The free-lancer (or staff reporter) will write it his way to suit his own needs. He is well aware of the publicity value of the story, but his interest lies in what you can do for him, not the other way around.

If you have something of regional or national interest, you are a likely candidate for a magazine feature. But you don't have to wait around holding your breath for a free-lancer to get the message. Most areas have local writers' groups. With a little research and networking, you can find out who might be interested in doing a story on you. A press kit, news release, or phone call may net you space in a national publication. Whether a story is done, of course, is up to the individual writer's (and the magazine editor's) discretion.

The alternative to finding a free-lance writer is to find an editor and let him do the finding for you. If you have information important to your field, write a letter to the editor of a magazine that caters to your craft. You need not give away secrets at this point; be only as specific as necessary. If the editor deems it of value to his magazine, he will assign a staff or free-lance writer to do the story.

Do you have writing skills? If so, use them to your advantage. The most successful craftspersons are those with a reputation. Naturally, you are an authority on your craft. Boost your reputation by writing about what you know, which is your business. If you have something worthwhile to share with others in your field, and can convey that message clearly, magazine editors are eager to hear from you.

In the end it is all publicity. And publicity gives you name familiarity. People sooner will buy from people they know than from people they don't.

Desktop Publishing

The personal computer has changed the way millions of people all over the world do business. As power and versatility have increased, the price of hardware and software has come down to a level that has made the personal computer more and more accessible to just about everyone. Craftspersons can take generous advantage of what computing has to offer. Whether you use an Apple Macintosh or an IBM PC or compatible, you can put your computer to use in just about every aspect of your business from product and booth design to keeping track of customers and show schedules to bookkeeping and bill paying (see chapter 8).

Aside from taking the drudgery out of many of the everyday tasks associated with any business, the computer has granted newfound power to individuals in the form of desktop publishing. It wasn't too long ago that the phrase "desktop publishing" didn't exist. Publishing was the realm of newspapers, magazines, and books. And of course there were scads of obscure tracts, poems, and underground literature duplicated on crude presses and mimeograph machines. Today, it's unlikely that anyone with something to say would use anything but a computer to compose, design, print, and, with the help of a mailing database, distribute his words, no matter what they are.

All the popular word-processing applications have a degree of design capabilities, giving you control over hundreds of available type styles and sizes, and they even offer some drawing functions. You can design your own letterhead, price lists, invitations, business cards, and promotional material.

Software referred to as works programs—ClarisWorks and Microsoft Works, for example—has integrated word-processing, graphics, and spreadsheet applications bundled together and is relatively inexpensive. More costly programs such as QuarkXPress and PageMaker are highly sophisticated layout and design applications.

With a laser or ink-jet printer you can print your own materials. For large runs, you can take your camera-ready copy to a print shop and have high-speed photocopies or offset copies made. And for high-end, color brochures with photographs on slick paper, you can take your layout on a floppy disk to a printer to have the photos scanned and separated and dropped right into your layout—all electronically.

Marketing Research

When a craftsperson starts a business it is unlikely that much practical consideration is given to marketing research. The craftsperson has a product to sell to whoever will buy it. If enough people buy, the business grows. But suppose the product doesn't sell, or a popular item no longer moves as it had. The craftsperson who wants to stay in business has no choice but to find some other means of keeping the refrigerator stocked and the rent paid.

In the beginning little is at stake. You show your face to the world and offer it your creations. In a sense this is marketing research at its basic level, but it's disguised as the ultimate test of success or failure, a shot in the dark. It's either sell or sell out. As your business grows, and you become more dependent on it, you can no longer afford to shoot anywhere but in the light of day. Consider the potter, fairly well established in the wholesale world, who hit upon a hot new idea. It was so hot he went into full production, going so far as to buy a new kiln and hire help. He took his samples to a trade show, where he made a surprising and devastating discovery. What he believed to be a sure thing was a dud with buyers. It took three years to liquidate his "hot" stock at break-even prices.

If the potter had done a little research, he would have discovered in advance what he painfully learned in the end: Sometimes gambles don't pay off. The first step in any research project is to define the problem or objective. The clearer you are regarding what you want to achieve, the easier the gathering of information will be.

Product and market research includes the following steps:
- determining acceptance of and testing new products
- studying competitive products
- determining new uses for old products
- noting any customer dissatisfaction
- simplifying or expanding your product line
- analyzing the size of the market for existing products
- estimating demand for new products
- studying trends in the market

Research on advertising includes these tasks:
- evaluating advertising effectiveness
- analyzing competitive advertising practices
- selecting the right media

Gathering Information

Three methods of gathering information are the survey, experimentation, and observation. All can be applied to various areas of research. For a small crafts business, a formal *survey* is of little use. Making cold calls to buyers (calling people at random from a phone list) or mailing elaborate questionnaires is simply impractical, especially where designs and concepts are concerned. An informal survey, however, may prove beneficial. If you have a prototype or a few selected early pieces of a product, take them around and ask potential buyers for an opinion. You'll know soon enough the item's potential.

The *experimentation* method involves actual test marketing. Take some samples to a variety of local outlets and explain your intention to the owners. Offer to place two or three pieces on consignment for a limited time, perhaps at better-than-usual terms for added incentive. What's important here is to have more than one item in place simply to cut down on the fluke factor (a one-in-a-thousand sale will tell you nothing). If the product does well, you may be in, not only with a good marketable idea, but with some new accounts, too.

Observation takes experimentation a step further. Here you visit the store at a peak buying time. Watch people's reactions, or lack thereof, to your product. Notice which kinds of shoppers are attracted to it and which pay it no attention. This will give you a keen appreciation of who your retail buyers really are.

Many craftspersons have their own galleries or outlets and so instinctively employ all three methods. As a gallery owner you understand and appreciate more how trade-show buyers make decisions. One of the best places for a gallery is in a high-traffic tourist area. Here, you have an opportunity to observe the reactions of people from all over the country.

Another fine place for marketing research is the retail crafts fair. Even some veteran wholesalers regularly use this medium to keep in touch with the consumer. Retail crafts sellers are the first to appreciate the fickleness of the market and realize the value of keeping pace with it.

Of Trends and Trendiness
Discovering and keeping pace with market trends are important to any business. Market research in the form of trend-watching requires a more eclectic approach, as trends are based on dozens of disparate factors. Do not confuse "trend" with "trendy." *Trend* deals with movement and direction. *Trendy* means current fashion and fads. Trends move like rivers. Some are fast and turbulent, others are slow and meandering. But they are consistent and always there, always advancing. What's trendy moves like rivulets after a heavy spring rain. Eventually they dry up and disappear, sometimes into thin air, other times into the trend of the river. They are ephemeral.

Consider the gasoline shortage of 1974. This caused a trend toward smaller cars and more efficient engines that are here to stay. And remember macramé, tole painting, and découpage? These once trendy country crafts have been stored away in the attic of craft memories.

Today, items with a western theme are enjoying increasing popularity. The same is true for crafts with environmental and ethnic themes. Also, many craftspersons are taking advantage of the fact that gardening has become the number-one hobby in America. But what about tomorrow?

The popularity of kaleidoscopes was once phenomenal. Kaleidoscope makers were among those reaping the highest sales at trade shows. Unlike macramé, however, these beautiful items still have a place in the crafts world, and it isn't likely that they will be relegated to the crafts attic anytime soon. They are part of the powerful trend of contemporary crafts. They also are part of the trend of elegant "executive" gifts.

But how do you keep a finger on trends? Watching and listening is one way. Another way is keeping an eye on the business world at large. Study such magazines as *American Demographics, INC.*, and *Entrepreneur*. Aside from offering other valuable business information, they are repositories of information about society's movement and direction, about its wants and needs, about who buys what and why.

One trend worth watching is something many reading these words have been part of in one way or another, consciously or unconsciously, since birth. It's one Madison Avenue has catered to and exploited since the end of World War II: the baby boom. This "pig in a python" has been the most influential factor in marketing for decades and will not go away until the snake has finished its slow digestive process. First it was cornflakes and coonskin caps, then clothes and cosmetics, then classy cars and condominiums. And it's no accident that Tony the Tiger, once confined to Saturday morning cartoon shows, now can be found during prime time bragging that Sugar Frosted Flakes have "the taste kids have grown to love." The term *the graying of America* is a euphemism for the fact that the baby boomers are getting older.

Baby boomers are the largest bloc of consumers in the country, with the most discretionary income. They are the kaleidoscope buyers, the buyers of art and other beautiful things. They are the buyers of crafts.

And what about when the dust settles? Even now the boomlets are entering the market. What will their wants and needs be? Vigilance in trend-watching will provide the answers.

6

At the Show

THE DAY HAS ARRIVED. It's half an hour before the gates open. The arena is full of light and color. The hundreds of booths, row upon row of them, appear as so many storefronts. There are crafts of every description. Trade-show veterans appear casual and comfortable as they stand in their booths and chat amiably with their neighbors. They renew old friendships, comment on new merchandise, pass compliments on new booth designs and exhibits. A twinge of envy stirs the butterflies that have been settling in your stomach over the past few days.

Suddenly you remember a dream of the night before. You were in your booth, the trade-show floor was crowded with buyers, all of whom ignored you and your booth. You did not understand why until you looked at your exhibit. All of your carefully crafted samples lay shattered on their shelves. Undaunted, you scooped up a shard, rushed into the aisle and grabbed a buyer by the arm.

"What do you think?" you shouted. "Isn't this great?"

The buyer paused and considered your presentation. "Hmmm," he said thoughtfully. "It's nice, but I don't think it's quite what I need for my gallery. Maybe some other time."

Your rejection complete, you slunk back to your booth, where you watched fellow craftspersons exchanging goods for fistfuls of cash. You asked yourself over and over, "What do they want, what do the buyers want?"

Now, in a flash of panic, you turn to your exhibit to discover with overwhelming relief that everything is indeed fine. The show promoter, whom you met briefly yesterday, strides confidently down the aisle, pausing now and then to talk with exhibitors. Now she pauses in front of your booth. "Nice, very nice," she says as she eyes your wares. "It's going to be a great show. Good luck." And she bustles off again.

Satisfied you are in the right place at the right time, you relax. You make last-minute adjustments to your display, fan out your sales literature on the table for the sixth time. You look up to see several people walking down the aisle. They wear badges identifying each as "Buyer."

It's show time.

What Buyers Want

The chief purpose for a buyer attending a show is, of course, to buy. Craftspersons, buyers, and show promoters have a symbiotic relationship. Craftspersons want to show their wares to as large an audience as possible, buyers want handmade crafts to fill their galleries and shops, promoters want to bring as many buyers and craftspersons together as possible in an atmosphere conducive to sales. One group's success spells success for all groups. But all have a more basic need: to earn a living.

You go shopping because you have a want or a need. Perhaps it's a pair of shoes you're after. This much you know. When you set off for the shoe store, however, you may not know exactly what kind of shoes you will buy. And, as often happens, you might end up purchasing along with the shoes something you had no idea you wanted or needed. The same is true for the crafts buyer.

Crafts buyers know their stores and their clients. They have a general idea of what they can and will sell and what they can't and won't. Sometimes buyers get their shopping done quickly, for they have studied catalogs and preshow promotions and know exactly which booths they will visit. Sometimes they have just an idea of what they want and will only know for sure when they see it.

This presents a sort of double-bind situation for the craftsperson, especially after all the emphasis on market research and studies of demand. It seems that, to ensure success, craftspersons must stick to the same old themes and designs to give buyers what they want at the expense of embarking on new frontiers. On the contrary, however buyers want and need innovation. Just as they rely on the staples of the crafts world, they also rely on the new and different to give added distinction to their businesses.

But one of the biggest mistakes craftspersons can make is not identifying their market. To make up for it, they offer a wide and diverse array of goods, hoping to be all things to all buyers. What buyers want is a cohesive line of products to choose from, not a smorgasbord. They come to the trade show for diversity, to the craftsperson for specifics. When a buyer visits your booth, you don't want to present him with an overwhelming assortment of goods. He doesn't want to see a forest, he wants to focus on the best one or two trees in it.

On the other hand, a booth that is too sparse looks empty and without enough to offer. Step away from your booth and try to see it as a buyer would.

Once a buyer sees something he's interested in, he automatically registers an expected retail price then halves it. If your wholesale price is within a reasonable margin of his estimate, you might have a sale. Buyers want to know, as soon as possible, what your price points are. If your booth is not busy, he can walk right up and inquire. But if it is busy, what then?

He has to wait his turn—just to see if the price is right. Buyers want displays with wholesale prices clearly marked.

Even if your prices are clearly marked, there is something else you can do to make the buyer's job easier and faster. Have preprinted order forms readily available so that the buyer can begin filling one out while waiting to talk with you.

Exclusivity

Where possible, journalists seek exclusivity in interviews and stories. This ensures that they will scoop the competition. Buyers, too, seek exclusivity from their crafts suppliers.

Exclusivity guarantees that one buyer is the sole representative of a craftsperson's work (or line of products) in a specific geographical area. Exclusivity clauses in sales contracts cover several aspects a craftsperson should be aware of. Signing a contract for exclusive rights can enhance a buyer-seller relationship as well as put the craftsperson on firm footing in a geographical area. Because competition is thus restricted, buyers may be inclined to order more of your work. Exclusivity also can tie up your work in a certain area and even keep you from competing with the retailer.

An obvious question: "If I can sell fifty pieces to buyer A with exclusivity, why is that so different from selling ten pieces each to buyers A, B, C, D, and E without exclusivity?" The answer might be "Nothing is different," especially if you will reach a larger and more varied market, and competition is fair and equitable.

Competition, or the control of it, is a key factor in exclusivity arrangements. As everyone knows, competition serves as a consumer watchdog. In a perfect market, prices stabilize just as water, once agitated, seeks a level surface. Few markets, however, are perfect. Take, for example, the maker of wooden toys who painstakingly turns all of his wheels on a lathe. He cannot compete head to head with the toymaker who imports factory-made wheels.

Few businesses willingly seek out competition, and crafts businesses are no exception. If competition is the servant of the consumer, and exclusivity is the friend of the retailer, then who is on the side of the maker? Where exclusivity is concerned, the craftsperson can rely on a good contract.

Although exclusive rights work in favor of the retailer, they can benefit the craftsperson as well. But the craftsperson first must ask, "What's in it for me?" Presumably the buyer seeking exclusivity will work harder promoting your work. Be sure the terms of promotion are spelled out. You may be able to include in the clause the right of approval of advertising and promotional material as well as retail price. Because an exclusivity clause puts you under certain restraints, it also can be turned in your favor if it requires the store to purchase a certain volume of merchandise from you.

Carefully consider the time period of the agreement and the geographical area in which it is in effect. Keep the time period short—no more than a year. You can always renew the contract, but you don't want a time restriction to keep you from growing. So, too, with a geographical restriction. In a small town, geographical exclusivity can be fine. But where a contract covers an entire metropolitan area, it can be a disaster. Better to seek limitations in smaller chunks of the city.

There is a particular problem when you live in the same area as the exclusive buyer. You may be prevented from selling retail or wholesale from your shop or studio. The clause also might stipulate that you may sell only a certain number of items, or that you must pay a commission on any sales you make to the party holding exclusive rights. Read the contract carefully and make sure you understand all its provisions.

The Art of Exhibiting Crafts

In the 1960s and 1970s, when crafts celebrated its comeback, the typical exhibit consisted of work laid out on a couple of rustic barn boards across a pair of sawhorses or the rungs of two stepladders. Such a booth is simple and still effective in some settings. But new standards of professionalism have rendered this primitive form of display a cliché. Professional craftspersons now spend hours of design and construction time on their booths and displays.

Trade shows have been big business for years, and there are hundreds of firms whose sole occupation is designing and building booths and exhibits. They range from collapsible backdrops that can be stowed in a single, lightweight case to massive affairs packed in dozens of custom-made crates that fill a trailer.

Booths designed for retail fairs are not always appropriate for the trade-show floor. In some cases they are not allowed. This presents a problem for craftspersons unfamiliar with trade-show booths. Booth spaces at trade shows typically are eight-by-ten, eight-by-fifteen, ten-by-ten, and ten-by-fifteen feet. The larger shows separate these spaces by pipe-and-drape parti-

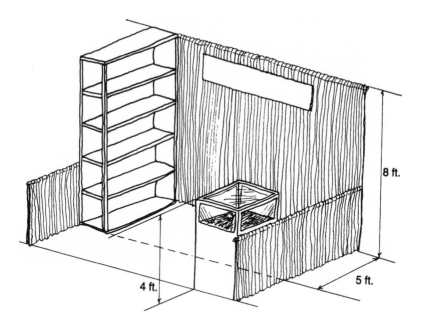

Typical Booth Restrictions. Generally, no display element may exceed eight feet in height so as not to impose on the aesthetic value of the booth directly behind. When side partitions are three feet tall, design elements taller than four feet are restricted to an area within five feet of the rear partition to ensure an adequate line of sight down the aisle from any one booth. Check with show management for specific restrictions.

tions, generally eight feet tall at the back and sides. In some cases the side partitions are about three feet high.

Typical Booth Layout

The simplest booths make use of the drapery provided by show management as their sole enclosure. In this case, exhibitors use pedestals, tables, showcases, and other stand-alone fixtures. If your booth is freestanding and complete unto itself, it must fit within the pipe-and-drape enclosure. For example, a nominal eight-by-ten-foot booth will be an actual seven and a half by nine and a half feet.

Some shows have definite guidelines on booth layout. Others are more lenient when it comes to physical character-istics of design. In general, all display materials are confined to eight feet in height. This is so as not to detract from the appearance of the booth immediately behind. Another height restriction may require that fixtures taller than four feet be placed within five feet of the back wall of the booth. The intent here is to allow a reasonable line of sight down the aisle. Such restrictions vary among the shows, so check the specifications carefully.

Do Products Really Sell Themselves?

A sales axiom: The product must sell itself. If this were com-pletely true there would be no advertising, no promotions, no glitzy showrooms, no fast-talking salesmen, no Madison Avenue, no trade shows. The primary function of all of these channels is to present the product to the public. Consider your booth another channel. Any product has a better chance of selling itself when it is placed in a context conducive to sales. The function of an effective booth is to display a product in an enticing way. A well-designed booth complements the product rather than competes with it.

Compare a jewelry store with a shop selling country crafts. Can you imagine a selection of diamond rings and pearl necklaces displayed against a backdrop of burlap with a few gourds and handfuls of straw scattered about? Can you imagine a collection of corn-husk dolls and whirligigs displayed in brightly lighted glass cases lined with black velvet?

These far-fetched and absurd examples illustrate the importance of setting. Your booth is your showroom. The best-designed booth shows off your products and allows them to do a little song and dance that says, "Buy me."

It's difficult to say exactly what makes one booth better than another; it's a matter of quality. If a design is successful, it works. If not, ask yourself why. Consider the cases of Exhibit A, Exhibit B, and Exhibit C. All three sit adjacent to one another at the same show, and each displays a line of decorative yet functional pottery. Each space is separated by pipe-and-drape partitions. Exhibit A consists of nothing more than a card table covered with a white cloth and a folding metal chair. On the table are as many pieces of pottery as will fit. In the chair sits the potter, looking hopeful. The philosophy of Potter A is that his products are so good they will sell themselves. Any additional sales aids only cheapen them and his craft.

Potter B has a different philosophy. He believes that while his pottery is the best in the show, there is so much competition from low-end hacks that he needs to attract as much attention to his goods as possible. His booth is draped in red, white, and blue. On the floor is an expensive Oriental rug, which he believes exudes taste. On the rug are several large pieces of pottery. Well-built eight-foot shelves of oak and chrome line both side walls and wrap two-thirds of the way around the back wall. Spotlights protrude from the tops of the shelves and angle back to illuminate the pottery. Some of the lights flash intermittently. On the shelves are no fewer than seven framed articles about the potter that have appeared in newspapers and magazines. Covering the middle portion of the back wall is a life-size, spotlighted photograph entitled "The Potter at Work." Also in the booth are two large round display pedestals with revolving tops. Toward the front left corner of the booth is a video machine showing a tape of the artist at work in his studio, complete with running commentary, which can be heard above the din. On the table in the middle of the booth is a large sterling tray heaped with club sandwiches. Potter B looks detached and confident.

In the entire right rear corner of Exhibit C is a set of curved, stepped shelves beginning at about two feet from the floor and reaching a peak at about four and a half feet. The shelves are draped with a heavy mauve fabric. Thick folds accentuate the pottery. One of the vases holds an attractive array of dried flowers. Behind the shelves is a brass floor lamp with a wide shade. On the walls hangs a selection of pastel florals. In the opposite corner is a low, round table with a glass top. On the table is a fruit bowl and several order forms, price sheets, and color brochures. Seated in each of the two chairs is a buyer. Each is writing an order. Potter C is explaining her technique to another buyer. She looks happy and satisfied.

Exhibit A represents the extreme of oversimplification. It suggests that its occupant is unprepared for the show or, worse, does not take the show and the buyers seriously. Exhibit B smacks of bad taste. The major problems here are that the booth is too cluttered and crowded, and the elements clash with one another instead of complementing the work. There is an overall sense of disorganization and lack of professionalism. To compensate, the occupant relied on sensationalism. Exhibit C represents a modest but appealing approach to booth design. The potter arranged her work in a gallery-   like setting, striving for simple elegance. She also provided for the comfort of her buyers with ample room in a relaxing environment.

Matters of Quality, Taste, and Judgment

Good design is more a matter of personal taste than universally accepted dogma. Yet clearly, some things work better than others. And there are a few guidelines. Display your most interesting item prominently; make it the center of attention. Keep your display within a range of about three to five feet off the floor. This, of course, depends on what you are displaying. The idea is to show things at a level for the most comfortable viewing by customers. But all things are not best viewed at eye level. Jewelry, if it can be better displayed in a waist-high case, is an example. A variation of this theme, which can't apply to everything, is to display things at a level at which they will be used. No matter how they are displayed, the product should be involved in the exhibit rather than added as a second thought.

Avoid a cluttered and disorganized appearance. Make the buyer's job easy as possible. Avoid the use of cuteness and gimmicks. Your exhibit must project an image of organization and professionalism. Don't skimp on the finer points. The first impression is important. Studies show that buyers spend no more than ten or fifteen seconds sizing up an exhibit. Your exhibit should help them make the decision to stop by and take a look.

Putting Buyers Where You Want Them

Another important consideration is where you want the buyers. Do you want to keep them out of the booth, or encourage

Many craftspersons, especially those with small items, choose to front their booths with a display counter. This method offers greatest security.

them to come in and browse? Some craftspersons, particularly those with many small items, prefer to close off the open side of the booth with a table, display case, or counter of about four and a half feet tall. Others choose a more open approach, designing the booth as a kind of miniature shop or three-dimensional catalog. Both methods have proven successful, but each has its own advantages and disadvantages.

The counter method gives you the most control over what goes on in your booth, and it helps keep your merchandise most secure. But it also can put real and psychological barriers between you and the buyer. The real barrier, of course, is immovable, but any psychological barrier can be overcome with salesmanship, personality, reputation, product, and other aspects of the booth itself. The use of a counter across the front of the booth yields much wasted space to the rear. Consider moving the counter in a few feet and placing two or three bar stools in front for buyers' comfort.

The open method gives you and the buyer more freedom of movement and offers more opportunities for enhancing the overall design. Having a chair or two and a table on which to write orders is always a good idea. This method also allows for more handling of merchandise, which can cause a lot of wear and tear. Overcome this by bringing along extra samples, should some need to be replaced during the show. Theft is another concern. It's a good idea to incorporate a locking storage compartment in any booth in which to stow valuables.

How your booth is designed and what materials you use depends most of all on what you have to sell. Will you need racks or shelves or a wall on which to hang things? Would pedestals or display cases better do the job? If there is any assembly to be done, such as for walls, light supports, or shelving, be sure everything is securely fastened and stable. During the show, a booth can take a lot of abuse. It can be jostled, bumped into, leaned against, and even windblown if a nearby door should come open at the wrong time. Having a display topple over can be disastrous for you and, possibly, your neighbor. Free-standing elements of the exhibit also

One of the most popular booth-design schemes at crafts trade shows leaves the booth open to browsing. Buyers are encouraged to step into the booth and browse, much as they would in a shop or gallery.

should be designed and placed in such a way as not to invite an unwitting surprise; all of us are klutzy at one time or other.

Light Shows

Lighting is a special consideration that baffles many exhibit designers. With the best lighting systems, highlights and shadows provide the necessary contrast to show off certain products. All modern show centers are well lighted to begin with. And that's often the problem. What looks dramatic in your shop or studio, where you have control over ambient light, could look washed out on the trade-show floor. Shadow boxes could help overcome this problem. In some cases, a canopy over the exhibit—if allowed by show management—will also help.

Sometimes more is better. Adding more and brighter lights may be just what you need to create the desired effect. But use caution. Where there is light there is heat, and heat plays havoc with plastic and other materials. Metal objects may become too hot to touch if a light is close and intense.

In Living Color

There is a television commercial in which a well-made-up woman explains that a computer has selected just the right colors for her to wear on her face. The implicit message is that it is far better to trust a machine to make our decisions for us rather than trust our own good taste and judgment. It assumes we will make mistakes in our choices, but a computer will never let us down. We also might pay someone, an " expert," to tell us what colors go best together. But the assumption is still the same.

Some people are more adept at putting colors together than others, but in the end it comes down to the mixing of a squirt of personal taste with a dab of good judgment. Most of us have a sense of which colors work well together and which do not. Sometimes it takes a little practice and some thought—putting one color against another to see what they do. That's what color chips and swatch books are for. Most often, color combinations that don't work (there are a few) are matters of personal and cultural bias rather than hard-and-fast rules. Exciting things can be done with color, when the emphasis is on contrast and complement rather than conflict and clash.

Stand Back

While at the show back away from your booth for a while. Step across the aisle and take a long objective look at your exhibit. Does it look, in the real setting of the trade show, as you envisioned it would? Or is something missing? Is it brilliant or lackluster? Are your products displayed prominently and dramatically, or do they seem inconspicuous and even hidden?

Watch people as they walk by. Notice how they respond to your exhibit and how long they pause. Do they examine the product, pick up literature, ask questions of your assistant, or do they simply pass without stopping?

Finally, walk around the rest of the trade show. Look not only at the booths of your competitors, but at all of them. Ask yourself what you noticed first and what path your eyes took as you first saw the booth. Which booths are crowded, which are not? Ask yourself why. Don't concern yourself with the products—some products are more attractive and popular than others. But if you notice two booths offering similar items and one's busier than the other, consider the reasons.

On any trade-show floor there are some booth spaces that are in better positions than others. Just ask the veterans who get first shot why they chose the spaces they did. And some spaces are worse than others, especially if they are stuck in an obscure corner out of the main traffic flow. If you are assigned a space that falls too far short of your expectations, the first thing to do (politely of course) is to bring up the matter with the show promoter. Cancellations do happen, and you might find an immediate solution to the problem. The promoter, after all, is on your side. If moving to another location is not possible, make the best of the situation. Most promoters supply floor maps for the convenience of buyers and sellers alike. Take one and customize it. Circle your booth number and add a note such as "Here I am. Come see me!" Describe your product. You can easily send photocopies in your preshow promotion if you know in advance that your booth will be in a backwater; hand them out at the door if you have to.

Salesmanship

One of the largest categories in the help-wanted section of major newspapers is Sales. Thousands of companies continually seek people with just the right qualifications to hawk everything from automobiles to zippers. Turnover is high in the sales world because competition is fierce and competent salespeople are few. Some people, seemingly, were born to sell; others were given short shrift when it came to that nebulous quality called *salesmanship*. The enterprising craftsperson need not be an ace salesperson to accomplish sales goals, but there are a few aspects of the sales world that can be of great benefit.

Selling crafts at a trade show, like many other forms of selling, is selling by confrontation. This does not mean that you accost buyers and browbeat them into buying. Rather, it means meeting them face to face to explain why they should buy what you have to offer. The advantage of trade shows over other kinds of confrontational selling is the number of buyers gathered to confront you, the seller.

Yet just being there is not always enough. You, the maker, have tremendous power to influence a sale. The object is to refine that power to your advantage. The major factor of your influence is your first-hand knowledge of your craft and your products. Buyers of American-made crafts—both wholesale and retail—are eager to know something about you and your product. A carefully prepared presentation of what you do and how you do it is invaluable. When you provide this background to the wholesale buyer, he in turn can do the same for his retail customers. In a sense you are setting the example, or standard, by which future sales of your goods are set. You also have the opportunity here to demonstrate various applications of your crafts that might not be readily apparent. People are always interested in new and different ways to use things.

Involving the Buyer

An important aspect of confrontational selling is involving the buyer in the sale. Encourage a prospective buyer to handle your product. Have him feel the texture and weight of it. If it's something wearable, have him try it on. If it's a musical instrument, give him a quick lesson. If it's something mechanical, let him see for himself how easy it is to operate. Your product won't sell itself unless you give it every opportunity to do so.

A word of caution. *Proxemics* is the branch of human communication that deals with the proximity of persons in a given transaction. Studies in human communication reveal four zones in which communication takes place:

- public (twelve feet and beyond)

- social-consultative (four to twelve feet)
- personal (eighteen inches to four feet)
- intimate (nine to eighteen inches).

The limited size of the trade-show booth automatically puts people—at different stages of a transaction—into one or more of the last three zones. All people claim as their own the intimate space around themselves. As people move closer together, they indicate a willingness to become more involved with one another, even if only on a business level.

When dealing with others we give hundreds of nonverbal, and usually involuntary, clues about our feelings toward the other person. These clues indicate the propriety of coming closer together (both spatially and emotionally) or the time to stop and even back away. Encroaching too quickly or too aggressively into another's intimate zone can be disastrous to a sale. On the other hand, as professional salespersons are well aware, gaining access to another's intimate zone is, in a sense, a victory over that person. Then it's only a matter of when to sign on the dotted line.

Note: Proxemics is another reason to keep booths open and uncluttered. It gives buyers a chance to ease themselves into a situation. A too-close booth tends to thrust buyer and seller, or several buyers for that matter, into one another's intimate zone.

Qualifying the Buyer

Involving the buyer provides you with some very important information—it indicates a level of seriousness. Professional salespeople call this qualifying the buyer. Not all buyers who come to the trade show have buying as their primary objective. They, too, may be there simply to maintain relationships or observe trends. They may be there just for the fun of it. And otherwise serious buyers may just drop by your booth out of curiosity. Maybe your jewelry attracted the attention of a buyer merely for personal reasons. If that buyer owns a gallery that focuses on pottery, your chances of making a sale are slim.

Begin qualifying the buyer by asking questions that require other than yes or no answers. Instead of asking, "Do you like this?" ask, "What do you like about this?" Just like any other person, a buyer wants, in fact needs, acknowledgment. Ask qualifying questions about his business. "How do you think this product would do in your store?" or "How do you think your regular customers would receive this?" Of course it doesn't hurt to ask more specific questions about length of time in business, clientele, nature of shop or gallery (eventually you will want this information anyway if an order is placed). Another good qualifier is to mention that you have a minimum order requirement. Although it doesn't happen often, it's not entirely unheard of that a buyer is more interested in Christmas shopping at wholesale prices than placing legitimate wholesale orders for a specified volume of pieces.

You can judge by the answers how much interest the buyer has in your product and whether he is considering placing an order. A lot of times it's nothing more than a hunch. If you determine the buyer is not interested and is wasting your time, bow out of the conversation. Do it tactfully, however. The uninterested buyer may know someone looking for exactly what you have to sell, so it doesn't pay to be even subtly rude. Word-of-mouth advertising is a mainstay in the crafts business.

Each time you talk to a buyer, request a business card. On the back of the card note the buyer's qualifications as a potential customer. Develop an interest scale from, say, zero to five to rate buyers. Zero indicates no interest, five the greatest interest. Also note whether the buyer's outlet is appropriate for your crafts. This information will be useful later, when you follow up after the show (see chapter 7).

Ask for the Order

The most important question you can ask, the toughest qualifier of them all, is "Can I take your order?" Never forget to ask for the order. Simply asking the question may sway a hesitant buyer in your direction.

While working on a sale, it often is necessary to demonstrate why your product is better than that of a competitor. After all, part of your job is to convince the buyer why he

Your name				Sales order no. 00001		
Address				Page _____ of _____		
Phone no.				Date _____		

SOLD TO: SHIP TO:

Name _____   Name _____

Address _____   Address _____

_____

Phone _____   Phone _____

Terms_____   FOB_____   Date of shipment_____

Salesperson's signature_____   Buyer's signature_____   Ship via_____

Qty.	Stock no.	Description	Unit price	Total

IMPORTANT: Shipment complaints must be received within ten (10) days of delivery.
Breakage claims are not the responsibility of the artist. Report claims immediately to carrier.

The order form is a contract between buyer and seller and has all the information pertinent to the sale and shipping of crafts items. Preprinted order forms, as well as other business forms, can be obtained at any office supply store. Alternatively, you can design and print your own with a personal computer.

should buy from you. There is nothing wrong with this, providing it is done honestly and with respect for the competitor. Never, but never, disparage your competitor or his products. Not only unprofessional and unethical, the practice indicates a negative attitude as well, which the buyer may perceive to be a pervasive quality of your business. Another negative to avoid is apologizing for your prices; if you must apologize then your prices are wrong. And it doesn't pay to explain how difficult it is to make a living as a craftsperson. Most buyers already know this, especially those who are in business for themselves, because they suffer many of the same slings and arrows you do.

Positions, Please

Your booth includes a chair or two, intended for the comfort of buyers. There is no law, written or unwritten, that says you can't or shouldn't sit in a chair while tending your booth. But there is a psychological advantage to standing. It makes you look more eager and interested. Imagine a scene where a buyer approaches a booth and the craftsperson is seated, perhaps reading a book during the show (it does happen). The craftsperson looks up and asks, "May I help you?"

Of course you can help me, the buyer thinks. *That's what you're here for, isn't it?* So much for first impressions.

Body posture and orientation also play important roles in communication. In most transactional situations the more relaxed party is usually the one with the higher status. But a too-relaxed posture can indicate boredom. Bodily orientation refers to the position of the shoulders of the two people within the transaction. The best communication occurs when two people have their shoulders squared with one another and they are face to face (called vis-à-vis). As the shoulders begin to open into a V, channels of communication begin to close. The farther from this face-to-face posture, the less positive the communication. Transitions in communication are almost always accompanied by shifts in posture and orientation, no matter how subtle.

After you and the buyer have become acquainted, and it appears a sale is imminent, it is a good time for both of you to sit (never sit while the buyer is still standing unless it is to see to the needs of another customer or to take care of other business). This major shift in posture and orientation indicates an obvious, not to mention positive, shift in the transaction. People are content to stand while listening to others, but they usually are more comfortable seated while reading, writing, or closing a deal.

Personal contact is the most important aspect of salesmanship, regardless of the skill level. When buyer and seller know one another, and have developed a level of trust for one another, current and future business dealings are immediately enhanced.

Taking the Edge Off

Trade-show selling can be grueling, both physically and emotionally. If possible, take along an assistant to help tend the booth. It is imperative, however, that an assistant be as well versed in your craft and your product as you are. The assistant should be able to demonstrate the product, answer any questions, and take orders. An assistant who merely says to a prospective client, "I'm only the helper. The owner is taking a break, but he should be back in twenty minutes," is no helper at all. You may be back in twenty minutes, but will the buyer? To get the most out of each day you have to be alert at all times. You do not want to appear haggard or ill at ease. Frequent breaks, one every two or three hours, are often necessary to help maintain composure and comportment.

Sales Aids

Many crafts buyers are interested in the background of the products and the craftspersons who produce them. One of the best sales aids you can employ is the hang tag, attached to or packaged with each item. Hang tags describe the item, noting any special features, uses, or processes of manufacture. They also might include a few pertinent words about the maker. Hang tags are valuable sales aids for you because they are valuable sales aids for the buyer, who ultimately will sell your wares to the public. Anything you can tell the buyer about your craft can be useful in selling the craft at the retail level.

A big mistake craftspersons can make is not arriving at the show with professional literature. Just as the board-and-sawhorse booth has gone by the wayside, so has mimeographed and poorly photocopied sales literature. Competition has forced craftspersons to seek out ever more professional ways of presenting their crafts on paper. Four-color description sheets and brochures are becoming more and more popular. This kind of literature is expensive, but the cost is worthwhile because it projects a professional image.

All trade shows, regardless of the industry, are stomping grounds for literature gatherers. You can recognize them by their heavy giveaway plastic tote bags, one in each hand.

*Crafts buyers enjoy reading about
the origin and nature of crafts items.
The hang tag is an excellent way of
imparting this information.*

They visit each booth and collect as much literature as they can. Where this literature ends up is anyone's guess. Although most trade show promoters are vigilant in qualifying buyers before they enter the building, some literature gatherers do get by. This is especially true at shows that feature retail days open to the public. Be sure to bring enough brochures to satisfy some voracious literary appetites.

Price lists and order forms should be clear and easy to follow. Keeping these two items readily available enables buyers to begin writing their own orders if you are busy.

Another valuable sales aid is a step-by-step pictorial or actual exhibit of how your craft item is produced. This should be no more complicated than is necessary. Rely on the visual rather than on written descriptions. Take, for example, the woman who makes elegant cast-metal figurines. A simple revolving case holds a piece representing each step of the process beginning with the wax original and ending with the final product. You needn't give away trade secrets here. Nor is there much cause for concern that someone will steal your manufacturing ideas. If your craft item is simple in nature, it will be easy enough for someone to figure out how you made it and develop variations on your theme. If it is complex in nature and process, few people will be inclined to invest the money, time, and effort it would take to duplicate your process.

When it comes to sales literature, be brief. In the busy trade-show environment, few people care to spend their time reading. They prefer to see and to hear.

Video tape is becoming a popular demonstration medium. But its use can be overdone. Imagine a video machine every ten feet down both sides of every aisle and the cacophony that would create; hundreds of messages lost on overstimulated buyers struggling to tune out the incessant yammering. If you do decide on video, strive for perfection in production.

Two more sales aids that may be useful are volume discounts and display cases, but be sure your price structure can handle it. Though volume discounts may boost sales, they may not pay off in dollars. Whether you offer a volume discount or not, always establish a minimum order. Some craftspersons provide buyers with a display case or rack. These can be sold outright or offered free of charge for an initial order of specific size.

Finally, there's your business card. Make it attractive, as befits a craftsperson.

Checking References

Buying and selling at a trade show—where orders are written instead of goods exchanged on the spot—is a transaction based on mutual trust. The craftsperson trusts that the buyer will pay promptly when billed; the buyer trusts that the merchandise will be delivered as promised. It's a delicate balance between two businesses. When the balance is upset, the whole trade suffers.

Until a firm relationship between the two businesses is established there lurks that specter of doubt that one party or the other will not follow through. Consider the gallery owner with cash flow problems and deems your bill a low priority. Or consider the craftsperson who is overbooked and months behind schedule and can't deliver on time. Both reputations are at stake. News travels fast in both communities.

So what can the craftsperson do to ensure the buyer is

reliable? The first thing is to ask for *and check* references.
When you seek credit at a department store or a supply house
you are promptly given an application. You, too, can design a
simple form for prospective buyers to fill out. It needn't be
elaborate, but there are certain things you should know about
those with whom you do business:

    • buyer's name, business name, address, and phone number

    • owner's name and length of time in business

    • financial credit references (names and addresses of
financial institutions including account numbers)

    • names, addresses, and phone numbers of three or four
craftspersons with whom buyers have done business (preferably any who are attending the show)

    • authorization to check financial references

    Also, for purposes of market research, ask for a brief pro-
file of the business:

    • clientele (tourists, walk-ins, regulars, age group)

    • description of inventory (pottery, woodwork, jewelry,
high-end, low-end, etc.)

    • setting and atmosphere of store (mall, storefront, high-
traffic or low-traffic area)

    Some buyers, expecting such a reference check, come
equipped with photocopies of their references with further
information about their businesses. This is a good practice and
one that should be encouraged. If nothing else, it saves time
and eliminates a bit of paperwork at the show (conversely,
you can provide new buyers with a list of clients with whom
you've done business). Retail outlets with good credit are
willing to give references because they are eager to do business with you. Just the same, a presentation of references
should not be construed as proof of reliability. Always check
enough references on new accounts to convince you of the
buyer's reliability. It is not necessary to check references
before completing an order, but do so as soon as possible.

    Checking references may seem irrelevant, especially after a
friendly conversation, but it can save headaches in the long run.

Terms

Many sellers insist on COD (cash on delivery) or some percentage of the sale price in down payment before delivery of the first one or more orders on new accounts. Although this appears to be a good move on the craftsperson's part, many buyers consider this a nuisance and an inconvenience. Not only does it interrupt cash flow for the buyer, it indicates a level of distrust as well. And what recourse does the shop owner have if the merchandise is delivered—and paid for—but in broken or otherwise unsalable condition? Regardless of what buyers think about the practice, it makes sense to discuss COD terms with new accounts if you have any doubts about reliability.

The most common billing terms are "net 30," that is, the entire payment is due within thirty days of delivery (provided shipment is accompanied with an invoice; otherwise within thirty days of receipt of invoice). A variation of this is "2/10/30," which is intended as an incentive for quick payment. This allows the buyer to deduct 2 percent of the total bill if it is paid within ten days. Two percent may not seem like much, especially on a small order, but if the buyer has enough of these discounts available from other accounts it could add up to a substantial sum. On the other hand, the buyer may elect not to take advantage of the discount. It's a small price to pay for the use of *your* money for twenty or more days.

Terms are agreed upon at the time the order is placed. Also agreed upon then are shipping arrangements, who pays for shipping, and the date (or dates) of delivery. If there is a handling fee or other charges, now is the time to mention them. Buyers loathe hidden or added charges, especially when they discover them on the bill. They make their decision to buy based on your wholesale price. If the total cost is subsequently jacked up with additional charges, they are not getting the deal they bargained for. They may have been better off going to a competitor who includes all extra costs in the wholesale price.

Miscellany

So far this chapter has outlined the basics of selling crafts at a trade show. Yet there are many other minor aspects of the business that require less space but are nevertheless important. This section serves as a catchall, a tying of loose ends.

Unions

One of the first surprises awaiting the unsuspecting craftsperson upon his arrival at any of the major trade-show sites is The Union. Ever since the tumultuous days of the Industrial Revolution, when many businesses grew at the expense of the worker, labor unions have been a predominant factor in American life. Regardless of your political and social philosophies, labor unions are here to stay and must be dealt with. Strength through numbers is the backbone of the union, and it is with that strength that unions negotiate with management for better pay, better benefits, better working conditions, and job security. Members' job security is the issue that most affects craftspersons at the arena door.

All major trade shows across the nation are held in union facilities. Unions are stronger in some cities than in others. Which unions you will deal with depends on the city, the relative strength of the locals, and what they will allow you to get away with. Union labor costs $20 to $30 an hour, but this may not necessarily come directly out of your pocket. Check in advance with the show managers to see if they pay union wages as a lump sum.

Whether your exhibit arrives by motor carrier (truck), in your personal family wagon, or strapped to the back of a camel, laborers from the teamsters union claim the right to unload and cart your exhibit to your booth. A possible exception is if the exhibit is small and the elements few and can be carried by hand one or two at a time. Don't, however, bother looking for a hand truck or dolly to make things easier, because you will find a union laborer at the controls.

Once your exhibit is delivered to the booth, the carpenters claim the right to take over. They have jurisdiction over uncrating and assembling (as well as disassembling and recrating) your exhibit. Also within the jurisdiction of carpenters are the laying of carpet, draping of tables, hanging of signs, and other decorating chores. If your exhibit is one of several collapsible types or requires no tools or mechanical fasteners, such as wing nuts or bolts, you may be permitted to erect your booth with little or no union help.

Most booth spaces come with an electrical outlet of specified wattage, usually 500. Many come with a union electrician to plug in your lighting or other electrical system. Though this may not always be the case, prewire any electrical circuits within your exhibit to avoid additional charges. Also, if your booth has any wiring other than factory-installed, Underwriters Laboratory–approved fixtures (such as lamps), be sure to have the circuits inspected and certified by an electrician in your home town. Take the certification with you to the show. Regardless of where you exhibit, you must comply with local electrical codes. Because of the high risk of fire due to faulty wiring, the logic is sound.

Flameproofing

Ensuring that wiring is safe is not the only precaution facilities management takes to help prevent fire. Exhibitors are responsible for making their exhibits fire retardant. Be prepared for the fire marshal to turn up at your booth, pack of matches in hand for a flame test, before the show opens. Merchandise is excluded from this regulation. Flame-retarding products are available from major hardware outlets. You may have to hire a locally certified company to do the flameproofing for you on-site. For more information check with your local fire department and with show management.

Coping with Stress

Who among us is not familiar with stress and its effects on body and mind? The trade-show environment has its own host of stress-causing situations, many of which cannot be eradicated, others of which can only be eased. The key word here is *coping*. It isn't stress *per se* that needs coping with but the myriad stressors themselves, the things that cause us to feel stress. Control the stressors, control the stress.

One of the biggest stressors, especially for neophytes, is concern over monetary success at the show. You can only do so much to swing success in your direction. Nevertheless, the more immediate the need of financial gain, the greater the opportunity for stress and anxiety to creep in. Remember, financial reward is not the only form success takes at a trade show. Go to the show with the intention of making new contacts and establishing new relationships, gaining experience and exposure, and increasing your knowledge and understanding of the system. All these have the potential for stimulating future sales.

Preshow stress can be handled most effectively by research, planning, and preparation. Just knowing what's in store does much to alleviate stress. Procrastination often plays a part in adding to stress. But procrastination is a symptom of stress, not a cause of it. Stave off procrastination by making a schedule and sticking to it. Break large goals into smaller ones and tick them off one at a time and over plenty of time. Small successes accumulate into large ones. Success is wonderful therapy for stress—and procrastination.

But success is not a cure-all for stress. Indeed, success can also cause stress. The danger is taking more orders than you possibly can fulfill. Your alternatives are attempting to renegotiate shipping schedules or beefing up your operation with more equipment and employees, both of which may cause their own forms of stress. If you're not prepared to make such changes, when you've discovered you've written enough orders to fill your schedule, simply hang a sign in your booth saying "No More Orders." Then sit back and relax and take advantage of the other benefits of the show.

Coping with the rigors of the trade-show floor also can be tough. The din, the press of bodies, the constant pitching, the hours of standing on a concrete floor—all take their toll. Cut back on the damage by taking enough breaks to keep yourself sharp and alert. Only you know how much stress you can take before it affects your performance. Dress comfortably. The crafts trade is not one with a rigid dress code. Comfortable shoes that provide adequate support are especially important because you'll be standing most of the day. If you feel the need to put your feet up to get the blood flowing, do so.

A powerful stressor comes from above, if you exhibit in a hall lighted by halogen lights. Not only does halogen lighting, with its greenish cast, play havoc on colors in your exhibit, studies show it can cause headaches, blurred vision, and fatigue. Take frequent breaks to avoid overexposure.

If you're thinking that dressing comfortably and taking plenty of breaks seems an overly simplistic approach to dealing with stressors, you're right. Adequately coping with stress involves three senses not associated with the basic five senses of touch, smell, taste, sight, and hearing. They are the sense of commitment, the sense of control, and the sense of challenge.

Being committed to family or work or a cause or anything helps overcome a sense of alienation. Performance suffers when we feel uninvolved. We do things merely because they must be done, not because we enjoy doing them.

All of us need to feel in control of our lives and our destinies. A lack of control makes us feel like victims of circumstances, without influence over events affecting us. *Making* things happen instead of *letting* things happen greatly reduces stress.

A sense of challenge means an ability to deal with change. Things not within our control often force us to make changes. The challenge comes after we recognize we don't have control over certain situations. Instead of feeling victimized, search for ways to learn and grow from the situation. If you lack a sense of challenge, then change is a threat rather than a catalyst.

These aspects of stress management, of course, apply to every aspect of life. But since the crafts trade show is relatively simple compared with the rest of life, it is easy to apply the principles of commitment, control, and challenge to that arena.

Selling Samples

The products you bring to the trade show are samples of what you ultimately produce for the buyer. Unless you are attending a combined wholesale-retail show, you need bring only enough samples (along with replacements in case of damage) to adequately represent your line. Some show promoters allow you to sell these samples, usually at the end of the show. Other promoters forbid the practice altogether. Check with show management for policies.

Dealing with Large Orders

At the typical trade show, several buyers place orders with a given craftsperson. With luck the income from these combined orders will last the craftsperson a long while. And there will be enough diversity in buyers as a hedge against cancellation of some orders and slow payment on others. But consider the story of the fiber artist who received a single order so large the only way she could meet the demand was to dramatically increase her production capabilities. Based on the strength of the order, she negotiated a bank loan and began construction of a new studio. Before the building was completed, the order was canceled.

Though not common, such a catastrophe can happen. To guard against this kind of dilemma, insist that the buyer put half the potential proceeds of the order in an escrow account. This is an account with a third party, usually a bank. The money cannot be withdrawn by either buyer or seller until the merchandise is delivered. For both parties, it serves as an incentive and a guarantee.

While discussing delivery dates of very large orders, suggest drop-shipping. This breaks the order into manageable chunks that can be shipped over time according to a predetermined schedule. It keeps you from having to store a large amount of merchandise awaiting a single shipment. It requires more paperwork, but it also may ease the buyer's cash flow. This is good for both of you in the long run because smaller bills are easier to pay.

Cellular Credit-card Terminals

Anyone who's sold crafts at the retail level knows the importance of making credit-card purchases an option for buyers. It's true that credit-card companies charge a small percentage of each sale, but think of the dozens and dozens of sales you will not make without one. You set up the credit-card account with your bank. Be aware, however, that the old-fashioned machines that make an impression of the credit card are being phased out in favor of terminals that authorize and initiate the transfer of funds on the spot via telephone. This poses an additional expense for craftspersons, who are essentially a mobile lot. Crafts retailers who wish to make credit-card sales must lease or purchase a cellular-phone terminal, which includes the apparatus for reading the card's magnetic strip (some companies charge extra when account numbers are keyed in by hand) and printing the charge slip. These units could cost as much as $2,500. For purposes of reliability, get the best one you can afford. It must be powerful enough to send and receive transmissions from inside buildings.

7

After the Show

THE END OF THE FINAL DAY of the show has come. The doors close for the last time on the buyers who time and again made their way up and down the aisles. You leave the arena a changed person, wiser for the experience. You've gained new insights into the industry, met new people, got new ideas for improving your business.

Evaluating the Show

Ideally, you will leave the trade show with pockets stuffed full of orders and a happy tune on your lips. But do you know how well you really did? Was it even worthwhile? Spend some time as soon after the show as possible to evaluate the results. Go back to your list of objectives and reexamine them. How many promising contacts did you make? Did you learn anything new about the crafts business in general and your business in particular? Did you get any ideas for new products or learn about a new trend?

And did you meet your sales goal? Tally your orders and

check them against your production schedule. Will you make your costs? Will you make a profit? Will you have to do another show sooner than you had expected or take other measures to sell more products? Will you have to adjust your prices to reflect a truer picture of trade-show costs or to bring them more in line with the market? If your orders are short of your goal, remember that not all trade-show business is generated during the show. Many buyers place orders after the show.

Following Up

The show is over. You've gone home, walked through the door, and collapsed on the couch. But, to maximize what you've accomplished, there is still one more thing to do: follow up.

There are two areas in which following up is imperative. The first is with clients who placed orders. The second is with prospective clients who didn't. In the hectic atmosphere of the trade show, mistakes can easily be made. Mistakes breed misunderstanding. Clearing up misunderstandings after the fact sometimes takes more effort than making sure they don't exist in the first place. What's more, a valuable business relationship is at risk. The best preemptive strike against misunderstanding is confirmation. Within two weeks of the show, send each buyer who placed an order a note of confirmation of the order as you understand it. This can be a clear copy of the order form with all information regarding product, quantity, price, terms, delivery dates, and shipping costs and arrangements. Accompany this with a brief letter of purpose and ask that any misunderstandings be corrected at once. Otherwise you'll accept the order as it stands.

Many buyers place orders after the show. But it doesn't hurt to spur a decision or open a door of opportunity for a prospective sale. Here is where the qualifying of buyers plays a secondary role. Using the buyers' business cards you collected and rated during the show, make a list of potential customers and send them each a letter thanking them for stopping by your booth and for their interest in your work. Give a brief description of the work and its qualities as a reminder of what you do. Close by suggesting that, now that the show is over, perhaps the buyer would like to consider placing an order. Include with the letter a brochure, price list, and order form.

Customer Service

Service begins the moment buyer and seller greet one another. From then on the craftsperson, through ongoing good service, has a great deal of control over the future of the relationship. Providing good service simply means treating your customers well. It has been said that you can do everything wrong in business and still succeed if you provide good customer service; and you can do everything right and still fail if you provide poor service. Quality merchandise is the first criterion for good service.

Prompt delivery also demonstrates good service. If you can't meet your shipping schedule, tell the buyer as soon as possible so that he can readjust his own schedule. Sometimes it's the buyer who asks for a schedule change. Do everything to accommodate the request, short of putting off other customers.

Service also means problem solving. Does the customer have trouble selling a particular item? Why not offer an exchange? In addition, perhaps you can offer products and sales aids tailored to a specific client. It doesn't hurt to ask, and it could lead to new ideas and designs for other products.

In the end, good service always means keeping the customer satisfied. Guaranteed satisfaction almost always guarantees future business.

Shipping

The shipping industry is one of our economy's most valuable industries. It also is one of the most misunderstood. On a given day we may see a hundred trucks lumbering down our highways, yet few of us know what's behind the transporting of goods from one point to another. The world of shipping is full of baffling jargon and procedures.

For the craftsperson participating in trade shows, there are two phases of shipping to think about: shipping the exhibit to the show (provided it isn't carried in your own vehicle) and shipping merchandise to customers. The mode of transportation offering the best service depends largely on size and weight.

For smaller items the choice is between the United States Postal Service (USPS) and United Parcel Service (UPS) or some other privately owned delivery service. Generally, UPS is cheaper and faster than the post office and has a larger weight allowance. UPS takes parcels up to one hundred and thirty inches in combined length and girth, and up to one hundred fifty pounds each (some states, however, may have lower weight allowances). Packages longer than eighty-four inches are oversize and billed at a higher rate, but no package longer than one hundred eight inches will be accepted. Unlike the postal service, UPS will pick up from your place of business. You also can arrange for weekly UPS pickups (for a small fee) and an account.

Next on the list of transportation options is common carrier (truck), also known as motor carrier or motor freight, the backbone of the over-the-road shipping industry. This is likely the best bet for shipping a large exhibit to a trade show as well as large, crated crafts orders. Because of excessive handling en route, items should be adequately crated as assurance against damage.

Van lines (such as you would use to transport household goods from one point to another) are another method of over-the-road shipping. They offer individualized service, both for crated and blanketed (uncrated but protected by blankets) goods. A van line would be appropriate only for shipping large commercial exhibits from city to city. Air freight, because of its relatively high cost, should be used only in cases of emergency when time is a factor.

How much you are charged for shipping via common carrier is highly variable and complicated, but don't let these warnings deter you from using this mode when necessary. Though the best advice on this form of shipping can be obtained from local freight companies, let's discuss a few terms and conditions that may help untangle the mystery.

A *tariff* is a book that lists a variety of rate schedules and options. Tariff sometimes also refers to the rate itself. The *chargeable weight* is, as the name implies, the weight at which you are charged. It is *not* necessarily the actual weight of your shipment, however. For example, you may be charged by volume *in the van*, which has a predetermined weight assigned to it. The charge to you is based on the greater of weight or volume. The *break point* is that point at which it is less expensive to ship in a greater weight category, since rates begin to drop as weights increase. Weight rates are listed in units "per hundred pounds," which is abbreviated *cwt. Point to point* refers to rates based on shipping between two major cities. *Mileage* rates are based on distances between nonmajor points, whether origin, destination, or both.

When writing an order, buyer and seller must understand exactly what the shipping arrangements are. How will the goods be shipped? Who pays for shipment? Who owns the goods and is responsible for them during transit? How will the transfer be handled? The answers to these questions should be spelled out on the order form. The shipping industry uses the term FOB (free on board) to make certain distinctions regarding the shipment. FOB is followed by either a point of origin or a destination. Who holds title to the goods and when and where that title is transferred are indicated by the FOB designation.

Let's say your studio is in Portland, Oregon, and you are shipping to a gallery in Cleveland. *FOB factory* means that the buyer arranges and pays for shipping from your door and the buyer is responsible for the goods from the moment the order is picked up for shipment. *FOB destination* is just the opposite. You make the arrangements, pay the costs, and own the goods until they arrive at the gallery. *FOB Portland* (or *FOB shipping point*) means that the buyer takes responsibility once the goods are delivered to a specified point of departure other than your studio—a trucking company loading dock, perhaps. You pay any drayage charges to get the merchandise to the trucking company. *FOB Cleveland* is just the opposite.

FOB destination, charges reversed means that you own and are responsible for the goods until they arrive at the gallery but the buyer pays the shipping costs. *FOB factory, freight prepaid* means that the buyer owns the goods and is responsible for them as they come from your shop, but you pay the shipping costs.

The consideration of ownership is most important in case of damage in transit. Who deals with the carrier if there is a claim? If the buyer owns the goods from the moment they are shipped, then he makes the claim against the shipping company. That is the only way he will be reimbursed for the goods (unless you agree to replace them gratis with salable merchandise). Then he can reorder if necessary. If you own the products until they arrive at the gallery, then the dispute is between you and the carrier. You are still obligated to fill the order.

Also, always include a packing list or manifest in each box of the shipment. This list should have on it all items within the box and an indication of whether it is part of a larger collection of boxes, for example, box four of five.

Sales Representatives

Larger manufacturing concerns employ sales forces to get their products to the consumer. As salaried or commissioned personnel, they represent a direct cost to the company. The independent craftsperson has no need for, and indeed usually cannot afford, a sales force of any size. Smaller businesses, crafts included, have created a niche for another kind of entrepreneur: the sales representative. Also called a manufacturers' rep or sales agent, the sales rep works hard making a good living selling your items and the items of others strictly on a commission basis of 15 to 20 percent of wholesale. The more he sells, the more he makes.

If you are having no trouble selling what you make and can make a living at it, obviously a rep is unnecessary. But if you're looking to expand into new territory, or you haven't the time or inclination to be on the road much of the time, a rep may be just the person you're looking for. What's nice about having a sales rep is that he does the legwork while you concentrate on your craft.

Many sales reps come to trade shows or advertise there, looking for clients. They also advertise in the trade publications. Craftspersons, too, use these channels to find reps.

Sales reps, who usually work in territories, have dozens of contacts. They generally build their line with noncompeting products. Because they make their living at selling, they are selective about what they will take, staying away from products they don't believe they can sell. Sales reps also can work certain shows for you, but not all. Some show promoters require that the craftsperson and his assistants attend the booth.

The craftsperson's job is to provide the rep with sample products and sales literature. The rep does not buy these products. The rep's job is to seek the orders and turn them over to the craftsperson, who has the responsibility of fulfilling all of the other duties incumbent on the sale: packing, shipping, billing. Because the rep is paid only after you are paid, it is in the rep's best interest to ensure the buyer's creditworthiness.

As your agent, the sales rep represents you to buyers you may or may not know. What he says and does reflects directly on you and your business. Also, as your agent, the rep has the power to sign sales contracts to which you are legally bound. A rep can tie you up financially by filling your production schedule at the expense of your other clients. He also might place items in outlets where you may not want them. Though these are extreme cases, such problems can happen. Be scrupulous when selecting a sales rep; it is to your advantage.

One or more good sales representatives can be a boon to your business provided you establish the proper working relationship. Your sales rep should know as much about your product as you do. It isn't fair to ask him to be like you, but you can expect him to represent you in a manner acceptable to you. Because he also has a reputation to maintain, the sales rep should work for you and not against you. At the same time, you have a responsibility to make the rep's job as easy as possible with good product support and customer service. If you can't meet an order deadline, let the rep know so that he doesn't walk unawares into an embarrassing situation the next time he pays a call on a retailer. As a matter of professional courtesy, do not compete with your representative by selling directly to retailers he has established and cultivated.

8

On Paper

NEXT TO UNDERCAPITALIZATION, poor management kills more businesses year after year than any other ailment. It could be argued that the reason for a lack of capital is a lack of good management. Good management incorporates two distinct skills. One is dealing with people, the other is dealing with paper.

Paperwork has long been the bane of many a small-business person. This can be especially true for craftspersons who'd rather spend their time creating wares than crunching numbers. Fortunately, the home computer, along with spreadsheet and accounting software, has helped take the bite out of bookwork.

The cost of the home computer—whether it's an Apple Macintosh or an IBM PC—has dropped significantly over the years while its power has increased dramatically.

Sophisticated accounting software is relatively easy to use and displaces old-fashioned ledger books with their endless columns of tiny figures. You can easily track the course of every penny without having to sift through yards of adding-machine tape, and, with a keystroke or two, you can generate one of several different reports on the state of your business.

Spreadsheet software—such as Lotus 1-2-3 and Microsoft Excel—can help you determine prices, calculate material needs, and keep track of inventory. What's more, spreadsheet data can be used to generate a variety of charts and graphs.

As April 15 approaches, you can use your computer to help with one of the most troublesome chores ever devised—filling out your income tax return. Programs such as MacInTax and TurboTax take the drudgery out of the job and reduce what used to take several days to only a few hours. The software includes complete IRS instructions and all the necessary forms, which can be printed on a dot-matrix, ink-jet, or laser printer. Other features tell you which forms are incomplete and point out possible problems.

Although the computer has eliminated much of the paper in paperwork, the necessity of understanding certain principles remains. This chapter deals with the importance of developing and maintaining good paper skills, the behind-the-scenes work necessary to keep your business afloat and on course through the doldrums of slow months and the rapids of fast ones.

A Plan for All Seasons

Few mariners would set sail without charts to guide them. Businesspeople, too, need charts. One of those charts is the business plan, an elaborately prepared document outlining the history of the company, its products and services, management personnel, sales goals, competition, financial standing, and other pertinent details. Companies use the plan as a tool for acquiring capital from outside sources. For the craftsperson, however, such a plan has little use. For your purposes, the business plan serves as a way to consolidate your thoughts. It is analogous to working through a new design. The fiber artist makes a sketch, perhaps dozens of them, before beginning to weave. The furnituremaker first draws a detailed set of plans from which to work.

Unless you are seeking financing to start or expand, no one but you need see your business plan. Nevertheless, it's important to set on paper in concise language exactly what you mean to accomplish and how.

Integral to your business plan is the *financial forecast*. This gives you an idea of where you should be, or hope to be, over a long period of time. A one-year forecast is typical, but you can plan for longer periods as well. The three most useful parts of the forecast are the *income and expense analysis*, the *break-even analysis*, and the *cash-flow analysis*.

Income and Expense Analysis

An income and expense analysis, figured as accurately as possible, is essential because it gives you a year-end income goal to shoot for. It helps you decide where you want to be, or where you can expect to be, financially at the end of the forecast period. You tally your potential expenses for the year and match them against potential income. The difference is either net profit or loss. To turn a loss into a profit, you must do one of two things or both: cut costs and increase sales.

Every business has two categories of costs: fixed costs and variable costs. Fixed costs are those incurred by the business itself. They include studio or shop rent, salaries (yours and other executives'), taxes, and expenses for utilities, machinery, repairs, maintenance, general advertising, trade shows, travel, bookkeeping, and legal services. Other fixed costs to consider are interest on loans and depreciation on equipment. Depreciation is what you allow for replacement of equipment. It is not an out-of-pocket expense now, but what about later, when a piece of equipment needs to be replaced? Fixed costs, then, are those expenses not associated with production; they are the collective costs of operating the business. Don't be misled, however, by the word *fixed*. No cost is truly fixed for long, only for a finite period of time. Indeed, many fixed costs fluctuate widely.

Distinct from fixed costs are variable costs, which are *directly associated* with production. They include costs of materials and labor (employees). Variable costs rise and fall along with production. The more you produce, the more materials and labor you have to put into the process. Also included in variable costs are commissions paid to sales representatives, which are paid per unit, and some advertising costs, when they apply to specific products.

If you've been in business for a while, you already have an idea of what your fixed costs will be during a given year. If you're a beginner, you must rely more on estimates rather than actual figures. In any event, think of as many fixed costs for the following year as you can, list them, and apply a dollar amount to each one. Next, determine how much money you expect the business to earn that year. You should have an idea of both the quantity you can produce and the income you can expect to derive from sales. The determination may be largely speculative, but it should be as realistic as possible. The income and expense analysis, then, should answer the following question: "Do I have a reasonable chance of making any money during the upcoming year?"

Break-even Analysis

The second part of the forecast, the break-even analysis, tells you exactly at what level of production you will meet your costs. This is the break-even point. When sales go above this point you realize a profit. When sales do not reach the break-even point you have a loss.

To do a break-even analysis you need three pieces of information: fixed costs, variable costs per unit, and price per unit. Let's assume a total fixed cost of $30,000, a variable cost of $15, and a price of $25. (This example is based on the production of one product only. When more than one product is involved, the variable costs and price per unit figures would each be an average of all products.)

The break-even analysis is easily illustrated on a graph. The horizontal X axis at the bottom represents units produced. The vertical Y axis to the left represents both costs and revenue. Fixed costs are represented by the horizontal line drawn at $30,000.

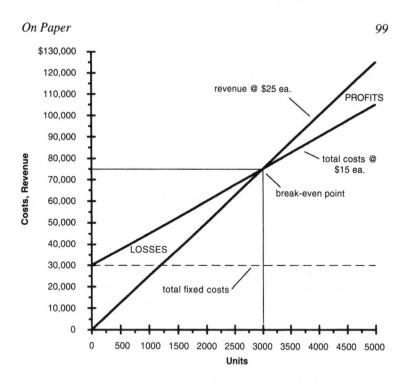

Yearly Break-even Analysis. The fixed cost line is horizontal because, in theory, fixed costs remain constant. The total cost line originates from the fixed cost line at zero production and rises as production costs increase. The revenue line begins at zero and increases along with production. The break-even point is where the total cost line and revenue line intersect.

To establish the total costs line, multiply each unit incre-ment by $15 and add to the result the $30,000 fixed cost. To establish the revenue line, multiply each unit increment by $25. The two lines converge at the break-even point. On the graph, the break-even point is the production (and sale) of 3,000 units, with a total cost and a yield of $75,000.

Notice that until the break-even point is reached, the $10 difference between the unit cost and the unit price is not profit; it represents the contribution each piece makes toward the fixed costs. Profit occurs only when sales surpass the break-even point.

You can plot your data on graph paper, but using a spreadsheet program with charting capabilities will allow easy experimentation with dozens of hypothetical situations.

Cash-flow Analysis

All businesses have their ups and downs, their good months and bad. The crafts business is no different. It's often a feast-or-famine proposition. A month-by-month cash-flow analysis can help you even out the peaks and valleys. *Cash flow* is the term used to describe cash coming in and cash going out. A negative cash flow means that more goes out than comes in at a given time. This, of course, is not good. The cash-flow analysis pinpoints those months with positive and negative cash flows. You are in a better position if you plan to use money earned during the fat months to help tide you over during the lean ones.

The difficulty, if you're just getting started, is that you have no idea which months you need to watch out for. Accurate cash-flow projections need to be based more on past performance than educated estimates. Once you have a year's worth of business behind you, you'll have the necessary data to begin. Tally each month's expenses and sales, then look for a pattern. Chances are the pattern reflects the major trade-show periods of summer and winter. Whatever the pattern, use the information as an aid in making cash flow work for you.

Setting Up Shop

Every business must have a base of operation. The facilities you need often dictate where you locate this base, and where you locate has a tremendous impact on your expenses. Fortunately, many craftspersons are able to work right out of their homes. This works for you in two ways. First, it reduces costs, since you already have utilities and will have no additional rent or mortgage to pay. Second, you get to take advantage of the tax deductions the IRS offers to those who operate businesses in their homes (more on this later, at the end of the chapter). By working at home you save money, which is another way of earning money. Imagine the pressure of having to earn an extra $1,000 a month just to pay shop expenses. Besides, if you do earn that extra grand, it goes into your pocket, not someone else's.

Another advantage to working at home is the time saved in travel. And as the saying goes, time is money. You save on meals, too, if you don't eat out.

Whether you work in your home or at another location, you are expected to comply with a host of regulations. Are there any zoning restrictions in your area? Will you need any special licenses or permits? Answers to such questions can be found on the local and state levels, but specific governing agencies vary from state to state. A few phone calls to city hall or the county courthouse should give you all the information you'll need.

Proprietorships, Partnerships, and Corporations

All businesses in the United States fall into one of three organizational structures: proprietorships, partnerships, and corporations. Each has its own liability and tax implications, which should be carefully considered.

The *proprietorship*, also called sole proprietorship, is the simplest form of organization and the easiest to start. In it, you (and, if you choose, your spouse) are the sole owner of the business and you work for yourself. You personally assume all the risks and liabilities involved in doing business. All personal assets are commingled with all business assets, as there is no legal distinction between the two. You (or your estate) are personally liable for any debts incurred by the business or claims made against it.

All business income is claimed on your personal tax return, Form 1040, with profit and loss calculated on Schedule C. Self-employment taxes (social security) are calculated on Schedule SE. Income taxes are estimated and paid quarterly, accompanied by form 1040ES.

Whether you need to register with a particular state agency varies from state to state. You may be required to file an assumed business name if you operate under any name other than your own.

The *partnership* is similar to the proprietorship except two or more people are involved. A partnership is simply an agreement between two or more people or parties (a corporation, for example, can be a partner) to do business for profit. Each partner has the ability to act on behalf of the partnership, and all partners are bound by any such activities. All liabilities and other claims against the partnership are shared among the partners; for example, the personal property of any and all partners can be seized by creditors to pay off debts. A *limited partnership* is a variation on the theme. Limited partners can invest in and share in the wealth of the business but are liable only to the extent of their investment. They are restricted from having an active role in the day-to-day affairs of the business, leaving that to the general partners. If a limited partner assumes an active role in the business, he or she also assumes the role of general partner, thereby losing limited liability.

The *corporation* is an entity unto itself, separate and distinct from its officers. Each corporation must have at least two officers, a president and a secretary, who also can be shareholders. When you organize your business as a corporation, you no longer are self-employed—you are an employee of the company. The company, then, must assume all the obligations incumbent on an employer.

As owner of a company, you have a double tax obligation. Your company pays taxes before dividends are disbursed, and you pay taxes on your personal income, including those same company dividends. The government has made a provision to ease the burden of double taxation on small corporations, called S corporations, and offers other tax benefits to sole proprietors. In the case of the S corporation, income is taxed only once, at the shareholder level.

Corporations offer liability protection, which is one of the things that make them attractive. For example, creditors can seize only company assets, not those of its officers or shareholders; therefore, your personal estate is protected. To ensure protection against liability, always be sure to do company business under the auspices of the corporation. When you sign a document, make sure you indicate your official capacity in the following manner: Roland Monk, President, Monkeyshines Crafts. Never conduct company business as an individual, and never handle personal affairs under the company name. If you find it necessary to borrow money from a bank, however, it's likely you will be required to guarantee the loan personally, thereby losing your protection in that case. Liability protection also ends if you commit a criminal act, even in an official capacity.

Each state has stringent rules dictating what is required for the organization and operation of a corporation. Specific documents must be filed, stock issued, annual reports drawn up, and annual meetings held. Because of the legal and tax ramifications involved in forming a partnership or a corporation, seek legal advice before filing any papers.

For further advice on business matters, contact your district office of the Small Business Administration. This federal agency, established in 1953 to promote the cause of small businesses, disseminates valuable information and advice on all manner of business-related topics. Furthermore, the SBA puts the Service Corps of Retired Executives (SCORE) at your service. This is an organization of retired businesspeople whose volunteer members are available for consultation.

When the Price Is Right
The Potter's Tale

Once upon a time there was a potter named Patrick. Patrick had a small business, which he operated out of his garage. He earned a modest living, but no matter how hard he worked, the business never seemed to grow beyond making ends meet. Almost every weekend he packed his van with pottery and traveled to a crafts fair, sometimes as far away as 300 miles. Once or twice a month he took pieces of his best work to a number of gift shops and galleries in his area, placing them on consignment.

One day, while setting up a new account at a gift shop, Patrick learned that the owner was preparing to go to a trade show. Patrick had heard about trade shows but had never given them much thought. To him, trade shows meant commercialism, something that was worlds apart from what he was doing. He imagined trade shows as some sort of bargain-basement affair, with people rummaging through inferior merchandise and haggling over prices.

"You've got it all wrong," the shop owner said. "At the trade shows I attend, the work is every bit as good as yours. in fact, from what I've seen so far, I think you'd do quite well."

Patrick decided to give it a try. Eight months later he found himself in a brightly lighted arena surrounded by pottery buyers from all over the country. He was amazed and gratified at how much the buyers liked his work. At the end of the second day, Patrick had a nice stack of orders. They felt good in his hand. Why, he thought, I bet there's enough work here to keep me busy six months, maybe even a year. And he was right. His production time was booked nearly solid. Just after lunch the next day—and with a twinge of regret—he put up a sign on his booth that read, "No More Orders."

That night in his hotel room he spread out his order sheets and began tallying the receipts. A year's worth of work, he kept thinking, I can't believe it. But three-fourths of the way through the orders his stomach began to tighten and sweat broke out on his forehead. Something wasn't right. True, he had a year's worth of work. What he did not have was a year's worth of income.

For the first time he thought about his job, his profession, and his craft as a business. He had always wondered why, no matter how hard he worked, he was just barely scraping by. "I just have to make more pots," he had kept telling himself. But now he saw that he couldn't possibly increase production any more. He reflected on his days selling at retail fairs, when he could keep the entire price of each piece he had sold. He hated cutting his retail price in half for these wholesale buyers. "How can anyone make a living selling at wholesale?" he asked himself. "If only I had all of these orders at retail, I'd be set. But if it's so bad, why do all of these other craftspersons seem to be doing so well?" Then it hit him. All the while he was breaking even at retail, he was actually selling at what should have been wholesale. Patrick was practically giving his work away.

The moral of the story: Poor pricing practices prevent potter's progress.

Notes on the Potter's Tale

How merchandise is priced—not knowledge and quality of craft—is perhaps the most important difference between the professional and the amateur craftsperson. There was nothing wrong with Patrick's work, which he executed with skill and finesse. But his prices branded him an amateur, and the buyers took advantage of him. Buyers know how much they can sell a certain piece for. In a competitive crafts market, with all things being equal, the retail price is generally set at twice the wholesale price. Say a competitively priced bowl wholesales for $20. The gallery owner then retails the piece at $40. In comes our potter Patrick offering a fine-quality bowl for $10 wholesale. The buyer sees that it's easily worth $40 retail and sells it at that price, which is certainly fair and ethical because as the legal owner of the piece she can do anything she wants with it. One way to look at it is that the potter paid the shop owner $10 to buy his bowl.

Because the amateur is unsure of how to set the price, he is unsure of the relative value of a given piece. This uncertainty puts him in a bad negotiating position. In fact, he is no position to adequately market his crafts at all. Some craftspersons even ask the buyer to set the price, putting both parties in a very awkward position. The buyer knows what he can get for your work, but he isn't going to share that information with you.

Low, noncompetitive pricing is one of the reasons professional craftspersons tend to shy away from some retail fairs, particularly small local fairs and bazaars. Another reason is having to compete with producers of low-end merchandise.

Buyers seek the lower prices and may even suspect your higher—albeit more reasonable—prices as gouging.

The professional prices competitively. The amateur prices randomly, giving little thought to the true costs of production. Often, the motivating force of the amateur is to generate enough income to replenish his stock of materials so that he can continue with his craft. And that's fine if the amateur is content to operate in a world of amateurs and hobbyists. But as soon as the amateur steps into the professional world of crafts marketing, not only is he in trouble, like the potter, but so is every other professional in his field.

Professionals understand pricing inside and out, from the top down and the bottom up. They know what they must charge to make a living and what they must not charge to avoid pricing themselves out of the market. In other words, their prices are competitive. The craftsperson who doesn't have a handle on pricing naively takes a wrecking ball to the competitive structure. This does not mean that craftspersons actively engage in price fixing. Rather, in a true competitive market, prices tend to stabilize within a certain range, dictated by demand.

Let's take a look at the potter's tale from a different perspective to see how unrealistic pricing can hurt not only the amateur's business, but the businesses of other craftspersons as well. Our potter, skilled though he is at his craft, is naive about how to set his prices. At his first trade show he offers price points that attract a horde of buyers who enthusiastically place order after order. He realizes that if he continues to take orders he will be unable to meet the obligations. Reluctantly, he stops taking orders, even though the show has one more day to run. He tallies his orders and estimates the income he expects to realize from an unbelievably successful first show. After subtracting his estimated production costs, however, he realizes that he will barely break even. The show was not such a success after all.

Also at the show were four veteran trade-show sellers who offered wares similar to those of our friend; their prices were about 30 percent higher. Their experience, though, was just the opposite of the amateur's. Because so many buyers scooped up merchandise at the lower prices offered by the amateur, the veterans saw a drastic reduction of orders for their own more realistically priced pottery.

This is a recurring problem for many professional craftspersons. Although they know that the amateur who undercuts the market—and himself—will likely be out of business in a couple of years, it is little consolation; there will always be someone to fill the niche. And now, many American craftspersons also must compete with foreign importers offering much lower prices. Hence the label "Handcrafted in America."

Pricing for Profit

Have you ever watched a clown shape an animal out of a long, thin balloon? He blows air into the balloon, but he doesn't fill it to capacity. He needs to leave enough elasticity in the rubber to allow for twisting and bending, room to make the animal fat here, skinny there. Otherwise, the balloon will burst. Pricing is like making an animal out of a balloon. You need to leave enough slack to be able to push here, bend there. The animal is your product, the balloon is your price, the air inside your costs. You can't fill your product with too many costs or else it will be too expensive to produce.

Determining the price of a handcrafted object—whether it's a production item or one of a kind—often can be a muddled affair, full of puzzles and variables. Some variables are more under your control than others. All of them represent, in one way or another, costs of doing business. Accurate pricing requires continual and meticulous record keeping of both time and costs. It also requires a healthy knowledge of the market and its trends, plus a strong dose of good judgment.

This chapter deals primarily with how to determine wholesale prices for your wares. But because the wholesale price ultimately determines the retail price, craftspersons who sell exclusively at the retail level will also find the information useful. Unless specified otherwise, *price* refers to wholesale price.

The price of any item, what a retail merchant will pay to own it, is made up of three components: fixed costs or overhead, variable costs, and profit. Fixed costs, as mentioned earlier, are the expenses of the business itself. Theoretically, these costs never change, especially over the short term. Though they allow production to take place, fixed costs are separate from variable costs. Variable costs, the actual expense of producing crafts, are wages and material costs, and these fluctuate depending on how much or how little is produced. Sometimes they are referred to as direct costs.

Although profit is not an actual cost to you, it is a cost to those to whom you sell. There are several ways to approach profit. If you plan for your business to make a specific profit each year, then consider it as one of your fixed costs and include it in your calculations. If you want each product to earn a specific amount of profit, then include it as a variable cost in your calculations, or add it later to a predetermined base price. Regardless of how it's figured, profit is what your business earns for itself. (In the following discussion, profit is not considered a cost and it is not included in the calculations.)

There are two basic approaches to setting price. The cost-plus method involves working from the bottom up. With this method, price is based on the cost of producing one item, or a specific number of items, plus a profit. The second method, the market-based approach, starts at the top with price fixed at a point where you believe maximum profit can be achieved. An attempt is then made to bring costs in line with the price. Both methods assume relatively stable costs and continual production. Neither should be used without regard for the other. If cost-plus pricing yields a price too high relative to the market, business may suffer with a loss of sales. If costs are ill considered in market-based pricing, profits may erode quickly if they are used to subsidize production.

Determining Costs
Many books discuss the use of formulas to figure price. A formula is a concise way of expressing a concept, a precise way

of reaching a conclusion: a + b + c = d. Because crafts is a way of life rather than a means to an end, it is often difficult to apply a rigid formula to pricing crafts.

The formula itself, however, is not so important as the fundamentals and principles behind it. The craftsperson with an understanding of these fundamentals and principles, and the ability to apply them, has an advantage in the marketplace. This said, it's time to determine the values of *a, b,* and *c* in an effort to determine *d*—the price.

Part *a* of the formula is fixed costs. If you've done an income and expense analysis, you already know what they are, but some further elaboration may be helpful.

A salary is a fixed amount paid to you or others on a regular basis. Wages are variable costs paid to you or your production employees for work done, whether by the hour or by the piece. (Wages paid to a bookkeeper or to other nonproduction employees, however, are fixed costs.) As a craftsperson with a business, you take on a number of roles from designer to craftsworker to mechanic to secretary to bookkeeper. How you pay yourself, whether by a salary, a different wage for each job, or a combination of both, is up to you. But be reasonable. Deciding that you will pay yourself $100,000 a year right off may not be the best move for your business. In reality, craftspersons often earn much less than minimum wage on a per-hour basis. A forty-hour week is something vague, impractical, and certainly all too short for your purposes.

Whether you work in your basement, garage, or some other room, your next costs to consider are those connected directly with the workplace. If you work outside the home, overhead costs are pretty straightforward; you know exactly what they are because you pay bills each month.

If you work at home, however, figuring these costs takes a little more time and effort. First, measure the total square footage of your home, including the studio or shop. Then measure the square footage of your workspace alone. Divide the workspace figure by the home figure to determine the percentage occupied by the workspace. Then multiply the percentage by the other costs of operating your home that are common to the business—utilities, insurance, mortgage or rent—and allocate those costs to the business.

Total your yearly fixed costs, then break them down into a more manageable unit, such as a month, week, or day. Let's assume your total fixed cost for one week is $480.

Now for part *b* of the formula, the variable costs. Let's say you make jewelry boxes of wood. You have on hand a supply of different hardwoods, a bolt of blue velvet for lining, and a box of hinges and catches. The objective is to determine first the cost of the material going into each box. The next step is to determine how much labor is involved. Assuming this is a production item, it's easier and more accurate to figure these costs based on several boxes rather than one at a time. Before proceeding, let's make some other assumptions. You can make twenty-five boxes in one week, but to do so you need an assistant whom you pay $6 an hour. In one week your material costs come to $100 and your labor costs $240 (based on a forty-hour week). So your weekly variable costs come to $340. At $4 per box in materials and $9.60 in labor, your unit variable cost is $13.60.

Cost-plus Pricing

The cost-plus method of pricing provides a visual model of costs at any point of production. As an analytical tool, it enables you to break down and apply a cost per unit based on a specific number of units made. The goal of this analysis is to help you establish a base price, one at which all of your costs are covered. This model uses seven costs to help you analyze production status at a given time. The first two, total fixed costs for one week ($480) and unit variable costs ($13.60), have already been explained. The remaining five are unit fixed cost, total variable cost, total cost, unit cost, and marginal cost.

Unit fixed cost is the average portion of the total fixed costs incurred by each of a specific number of items. If you make twenty-five items in a week, then the unit fixed cost is $19.20 ($480 ÷ 25 = $19.20). *Total variable cost* is the accumulated unit variable costs. If a single unit costs $13.60 to make, then two units cost $27.20, and so on. *Total cost* is the sum of the total fixed costs and the total variable costs. *Unit cost* is the average total cost of each unit. It is derived by dividing the total cost by the quantity. *Marginal cost* is the cost of producing one more unit. For example, producing fifteen units costs $684. Sixteen units cost $697.60. The marginal cost is $13.60. Note that as long as the total variable cost rises in even increments, the unit variable cost and the marginal cost remain constant. The table on the next page depicts these costs for one week's production of twenty-five units. The graph illustrates the unit cost, unit variable costs, total fixed costs, and total costs based on the data in the table.

At this point, the marginal cost—which in the graph follows the same course as the unit variable cost—may seem irrelevant. That's because this scenario assumes constant fixed and variable costs and steady production at an optimum level; it is a "perfect world" picture. Realistically, fixed costs do change over time, and variable costs are almost never constant. Many factors can be attributed to wildly fluctuating variable costs.

Let's say you've designed a new box you want to put into production. Essentially, the first box is one of a kind, so production is slow, below optimum level. Your variable cost, therefore, is much higher, especially in labor. Also there may be a greater-than-average waste of material. Keep in mind, however, that as overall production increases, you will buy more material, most likely at a discount, which decreases your variable costs.

As you learn the most efficient way to cut and assemble the pieces that go into the box, production increases to the optimum level. Chances are it won't stay there. Production slows when fatigue sets in and machinery needs attention. An unexpected contributor to a slowdown is too much production. What do you do with all of those boxes, complete and incomplete, as they pile up around the shop hampering your progress? Overtime wages also contribute significantly to variable costs.

Simple cost analysis

Quantity	Total fixed cost	Unit fixed costs tfc ÷ q	Total variable cost	Unit variable cost tvc ÷ q	Total cost tfc + tvc	Marginal cost	Unit cost tc ÷ q
0	$480				$480.00		
1	480	$480.00	$13.60	$13.60	493.60	$13.60	$493.60
2	480	240.00	27.20	13.60	507.20	13.60	253.60
3	480	160.00	40.80	13.60	520.80	13.60	173.60
4	480	120.00	54.40	13.60	534.40	13.60	133.60
5	480	96.00	68.00	13.60	548.00	13.60	109.60
6	480	80.00	81.60	13.60	561.60	13.60	93.60
7	480	68.57	95.20	13.60	575.20	13.60	82.17
8	480	60.00	108.80	13.60	588.80	13.60	73.60
9	480	53.33	122.40	13.60	602.40	13.60	66.93
10	480	48.00	136.00	13.60	616.00	13.60	61.60
11	480	43.64	149.60	13.60	629.60	13.60	57.24
12	480	40.00	163.20	13.60	643.20	13.60	53.60
13	480	36.92	176.80	13.60	656.80	13.60	50.52
14	480	34.29	190.40	13.60	670.40	13.60	47.89
15	480	32.00	204.00	13.60	684.00	13.60	45.60
16	480	30.00	217.60	13.60	697.60	13.60	43.60
17	480	28.24	231.20	13.60	711.20	13.60	41.84
18	480	26.67	244.80	13.60	724.80	13.60	40.27
19	480	25.26	258.40	13.60	738.40	13.60	38.86
20	480	24.00	272.00	13.60	752.00	13.60	37.60
21	480	22.86	285.60	13.60	765.60	13.60	36.46
22	480	21.82	299.20	13.60	779.20	13.60	35.42
23	480	20.87	312.80	13.60	792.80	13.60	34.47
24	480	20.00	326.40	13.60	806.40	13.60	33.60
25	480	19.20	340.00	13.60	820.00	13.60	32.80

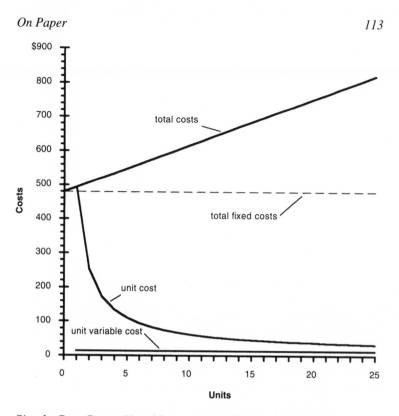

Simple Cost Curve. Variable costs are added to total fixed costs to produce a total cost curve. Total costs increase as production increases, but the cost per unit decreases.

The next table and set of graphs illustrate a more realistic picture. Notice that the unit variable cost and the marginal cost are high at the beginning of the production run but begin to drop as efficiency improves. Production reaches the optimum level at the tenth unit, when the unit variable cost approaches its previously established level of $13.60. Note, too, the significant drop in the marginal cost. At optimum production, the marginal cost levels off, while the unit variable cost continues to fall. At the nineteenth unit, the marginal cost begins to rise (again, for a variety of hypothetical reasons). This means that the cost of producing the nineteenth unit is greater than the cost of producing the twentieth, and so

Realistic cost analysis

Quantity	Total fixed cost	Unit fixed costs tfc ÷ q	Total variable cost	Unit variable cost tvc ÷ q	Total cost tfc + tvc	Marginal cost	Unit cost tc ÷ q
0	$480				$480		
1	480	$480.00	$20	$20.00	500	$20	$500.00
2	480	240.00	38	19.00	518	18	259.00
3	480	160.00	55	18.33	535	17	178.33
4	480	120.00	71	17.75	551	16	137.75
5	480	96.00	85	17.00	565	14	113.00
6	480	80.00	97	16.17	577	12	96.17
7	480	68.57	109	15.57	589	12	84.14
8	480	60.00	120	15.00	600	11	75.00
9	480	53.33	130	14.44	610	10	67.78
10	480	48.00	139	13.90	619	9	61.90
11	480	43.64	148	13.45	628	9	57.09
12	480	40.00	157	13.08	637	9	53.08
13	480	36.92	166	12.77	646	9	49.69
14	480	34.29	175	12.50	655	9	46.79
15	480	32.00	184	12.27	664	9	44.27
16	480	30.00	193	12.06	673	9	42.06
17	480	28.24	202	11.88	682	9	40.12
18	480	26.67	211	11.72	691	9	38.39
19	480	25.26	221	11.63	701	10	36.89
20	480	24.00	232	11.60	712	11	35.60
21	480	22.86	246	11.71	726	14	34.57
22	480	21.82	261	11.86	741	15	33.68
23	480	20.87	281	12.22	761	20	33.09
24	480	20.00	306	12.75	786	25	32.75
25	480	19.20	341	13.64	821	35	32.84

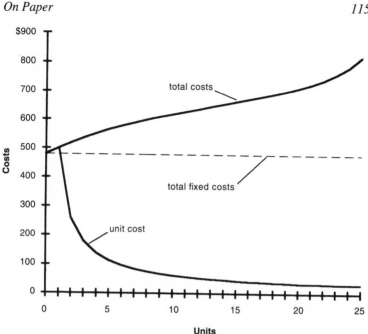

Realistic Costs Curve. Variable costs rarely remain constant, but tend to fluctuate during production.

on. Your unit variable cost is still on the decline, until the twenty-first unit. Your costs are still covered, however, because your marginal cost (the cost of producing one more unit) is still less than your unit cost.

But consider the costs for unit twenty-five. Your unit variable cost and unit cost are each within four cents of those shown on the sample cost analysis table. The marginal cost, however, is much higher. As the unit variable cost begins to rise, so does the marginal cost. When the marginal cost begins to move above the average cost per unit, the unit variable cost begins to increase faster than the unit fixed cost decreases. It costs you more to make item twenty-five ($35) than you can sell it for at its assigned unit cost ($32.84).

Once you have established your price point based on unit cost, you then can add the desired profit, part *c* of the for-

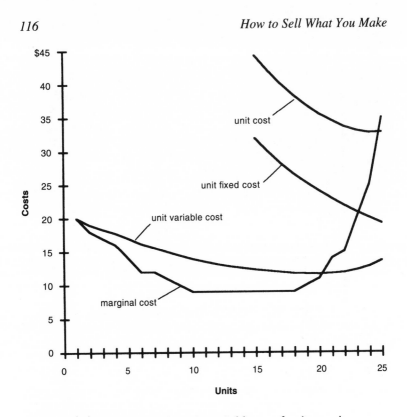

Closer Look at Costs. As the unit variable cost begins to rise, so too does the marginal cost. You begin to operate at a loss when the marginal cost is greater than the unit cost.

mula, to set your wholesale price, part *d*. This done, the percentage of the markup can be applied to other items.

In a perfect world, where costs, demand, production, and sales remain constant, cost-plus pricing is ideal. Few craftspersons, however, work in a perfect world. Costs do fluctuate. And you can never be completely sure of demand. (Of course, after you've written enough trade-show orders to fill your production schedule, you'll have a more concrete sense of demand, but by then your prices are already set.) Critics of cost-plus pricing argue that the method largely ignores market demand in its calculations.

When used by itself for pricing production work, and with

total disregard for the market, the cost-plus method is risky. For commissioned work or high-end, one-of-a-kind work where demand is nil until the piece is finished, it is far more practical. The value of the cost-plus model of setting price is twofold. First, it forces you to think in terms of costs. Second, it allows you to see exactly how these costs are affected by the vagaries of production.

Break-even Analysis Revisited

The break-even analysis enables you to see the point where revenues equal costs at a specific production level and at a given price. Items sold at a price above this point yield a profit, below this point, a loss. Used in conjunction with the cost-plus model, it helps you to set a realistic price and better manage your production schedule.

As with the cost-plus method, the break-even analysis makes several major assumptions. The first is that you sell everything you make at the price you ask. Second, that fixed costs remain static and total variable costs increase at an equal per-unit rate. Third, that you can accurately estimate demand at various prices.

Those assumptions point out the weaknesses of the analysis. Under conditions of widely fluctuating costs, the value of the break-even analysis is diminished because it tends to distort and oversimplify reality.

Break-even points for four base prices.

Unit cost $tc \div q$	Unit variable cost $tvc \div q$	Unit contribution to TFC (uco) $uc - uvc$	Total fixed costs	Units needed to break even $tfc \div uco$
$25	$13.60	$11.40	$480	42
35	13.60	21.40	480	22
45	13.60	26.40	480	18
60	13.60	46.40	480	10

Using data already established, this table shows the break-even point for four base prices (excluding profit). At $25 you would have to produce forty-two boxes in a week's time to cover costs. At that price each box would contribute $11.40 to your total fixed costs ($25 - $13.60 in unit variable costs = $11.40). At $60.00 you would have to produce just ten boxes a week, and each one would contribute $46.40 to overhead costs.

The $25 price is far too low because, in our scenario, producing forty-two boxes a week is impossible. At $60 produc-

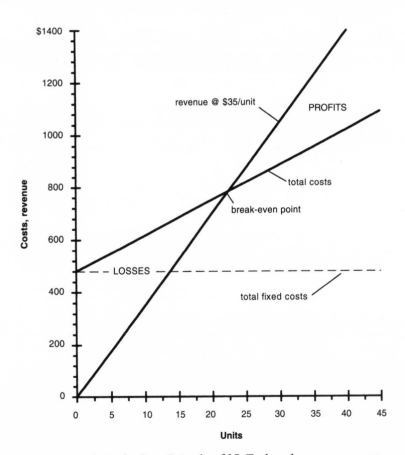

Break-even Point for Item Priced at $35. To break-even you must produce 22 units. This yields a total revenue of $770.

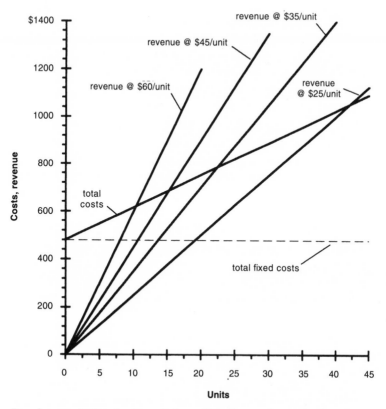

Break-even Points for Four Prices. This figure shows the break-even points for the four prices listed in the table. You can plot break-even points by selected price, level of production, or total revenue.

tion strain is eased. It is unlikely, however, that you can sell many of your ten boxes at that price.

A $35 price more closely fits the desired price range established in the cost-plus analysis. The first graph illustrates what this would look like on a curve. The second graph shows the break-even points for the four prices shown in the table.

Market-based Pricing

The cost-plus method of pricing builds a price from the bottom up. The other extreme is working from the top down, basing price on current market conditions. This form is useful when there is fierce competition and where there exists a traditional expected price range. This method makes the important assumption that once you've set a market-based price, you can then tailor your costs to fit within the range.

Suppose your wooden box competes with several others of similar nature and quality in the $40 wholesale range. Suppose further that your costs demand that you set your price at $60. Your choices are either to maintain your price at $60 or to reduce it to within the expected range. If you stick with the first option, you can expect to sell fewer boxes than your competition, if any. If you choose option two, it is imperative that you pare your costs to fit that range. In either case, your only real alternative is to take another job to subsidize your crafts business.

The objective of market-based pricing is to determine a price at which maximum profit can be realized. The first step is to determine demand at various price points.

If you can sell six items at $60, your yield is $360. But suppose you can sell eight items at $50. Your yield then will be $400. Twelve items at $40, the competitive market price, is $480. Perhaps if you cut your price below the competition's, you will be able to sell more items and, therefore, make up the difference in volume.

Pricing Potpourri

Thus far, pricing has been discussed in terms of formulas. Pricing formulas, whether based on costs or the market, are merely tools for the craftsperson and work best when used in concert with a large dose of judgment. Now is the time to depart from such rigidity, gather stray thoughts, and tie up loose ends.

Striving for profit over the long term has more benefit for the craftsperson than seeking short-term profits and sales for the sake of sales. It is acceptable, and sometimes wise, to take a loss on some items. The goal is maximum profit on the combined output rather than on the unit output.

Ultimately, you set your price to reflect the work you put into the piece as well as its other costs. The more competitive the item, the more the price has to be in line with the market. If it truly is unique, you likely will be able to demand a higher price. At the same time, so can your dealer. Don't be surprised if you find some items marked up more than 100 percent. Do be surprised, however, if it's less. Retailers who discount your work are underselling your other dealers. This is especially a problem if there are several dealers in the same area selling your work.

A word on markup: Wholesalers and retailers view markup differently. The craftsperson can think in terms of a 100 percent markup on the wholesale price. An item with a wholesale price of $20 will retail at $40. But retailers think in terms of a markup of 50 percent of the retail price (50 percent of $40 is $20). Both yield the same result, but they are arrived at differently.

People have a general idea of the value and price range of certain objects. For example, you expect to pay $800 to $1,200 for a standard refrigerator. This is known as the expected price. If the item were priced higher than the range, it would have to have an *apparent value* to justify the price. Adding apparent value, such as more bells and whistles, is a practice that lets manufacturers offer a variety of merchandise at a variety of prices. Consider also name-brand items, which are usually priced higher than generic brands. The *actual value* may or may not reflect the apparent value and quality. The same holds true for crafts. A buyer of handcrafted work will make a judgment on the expected price of a certain item. If the price is out of that range, the buyer wonders what added value or values justify the increase. One-of-a-kind work is a good example. Its uniqueness automatically increases its value beyond actual costs, especially if a craftsperson's reputation comes along with the piece.

Having an idea of the expected retail price of any items you produce helps you judge where to set your wholesale price. If the expected price is below what you can produce the item for, then you must somehow increase the product's value, or the apparent value, or both. You can add new features to the product, attempt to place it in outlets where it can be compared to more expensive items, or concentrate on an advertising campaign that will lend it more prestige. If the expected price is above what it costs you to produce it, you have great leeway to maximize profit.

Of course, from the craftsperson's point of view, there are two expected price ranges: wholesale and retail. Since the retailer has an expected range for items in her store, she also has an expected price for crafts sold at wholesale.

In general, a price should not be lower than expected because it would project a loss of apparent value. Take the example of the refrigerator. If you expect to pay at least $800 for it but the price tag is $500, you might scratch your head and wonder what corners were cut during its manufacture. A psychological disadvantage also accompanies a price below the expected range. A buyer's ego may prevent her from paying too low a price. And who among us hasn't, at one time or another, purchased a costly item instead of a similar, less expensive one with the belief that the more it costs the better it must be?

Once wholesale or retail prices are established, stick with them until you see a need to change them. Erratic price changes appear unprofessional. On the other hand, prices are always on trial, and changing them when necessary is no crime. As a rule, it is easier to work with a high initial price within the price range than a low one. If you find you must lower the price, you have the psychological advantage of creating a bargain. On the other hand, raising the price without an increase of apparent value risks the loss of goodwill.

By the Books

When you begin a crafts business, you will realize that the most important thing needed to sustain it is constant sales. This is the foundation of any business, and no business can survive long without it. A sale is simply the exchange of goods or services for dollars. The more exchanges, the more dollars. And that means growth.

Or does it? It does when the increase in dollars outpaces the increase in expenses. It doesn't when expenses keep pace with or outpace income. It's impossible to gauge the growth of a business (or lack of growth) by bank deposits alone because these give you only part of the picture. You need to look at the entire picture.

Only one way leads to the entire picture: record keeping. This does not mean making sure you put every slip of paper—receipt, invoice, check stub, or what have you—into a large paper sack for an accountant to figure out later. It means properly *recording* all of those transactions in neat little columns for your accountant to figure out later.

Two questions arise here. First, if you're going to do all that bookkeeping, why do you need an accountant? Second, if an accountant can straighten out everything anyway, why bother with bookkeeping?

First answer: If your business is small and uncomplicated, and stays that way, you probably don't need an accountant. But what is small and uncomplicated to one person might be large and cumbersome to another. And what about when things change, when business grows? As things get more complicated, you are bound to have more and more questions only an accountant can answer, especially about taxes and payroll. An accountant can spot potential problems, problems you may not see, and point out ways to correct them. What's more, an accountant can figure the quarterly reports and financial statements necessary for obtaining financing.

As you start out, an accountant can advise you on a number of topics that could keep you on course. Most accounting firms offer a variety of services from simple bookkeeping to tax preparation to management consultation. More and more firms are doing computer consulting, helping clients set up their own accounting programs and instructing them on how to use the software. Some even sell accounting software.

Second answer: Meaning no disrespect to accountants, they are like computers. What they can do for you relies heavily on the information you give them. Fortunately, accountants are people who, unlike computers, can reason and make judg-

ments about information they have or don't have. If at the end
of the year you turn over to your accountant a paper sack full of
receipts, check stubs, invoices, and all of the other various
slips of paper associated with your business, you will cause
your accountant all manner of grief. His first urge would be to
go out and purchase a good shredder. But he will sigh and begin
to assemble this mass of nonsense into sensible piles, then
steadfastly enter the data into his own computer. He also will
keep track of the time it takes. Time is money. Your money.

Adequately (and honestly) kept books do one more thing
than tell you the state of your business. They represent you
kindly to the Internal Revenue Service. If you are audited, and
your records are sketchy, the IRS may disallow some per-
fectly legitimate deductions on the basis of lack of substantia-
tion. The IRS is very particular about such things as a person's
income and the deductions he claims. Well-kept books—with
the receipts, invoices, and vouchers to back them up—tell the
IRS that you have the best of intentions. And if you happen to
make a mistake on your return—perhaps claim an illegitimate
deduction—and you are audited, the IRS will only disallow
the deduction, reassess your tax liability, and possibly levy a
fine. But it's doubtful you will be tossed into prison for fraud.

Another advantage of having an accountant in your corner
is that he can represent you to the IRS in case of an audit.

The cost of consulting with an accountant and an attorney
before you embark on a business venture will be much less
than hiring them to get you out of a fix later on.

Debits and Credits

Check writing, invoicing, and accounting software have
changed the way people keep books. No longer is it necessary
to keep a handful of sharp No. 2 pencils nearby as you enter
and tally column after column of tiny figures. Yet a rudimen-
tary understanding of traditional bookkeeping procedures and
concepts can be beneficial to both those who keep their own
computerized books and those who turn the chore over to an
accountant.

Books are broken down into three categories: the cash

receipts journal, the cash disbursements journal, and the general ledger. The cash receipts journal records all cash as it's received. Outgoing cash is accounted for in the cash disbursements journal. The general ledger is an assembly of these transactions in the form of accounts.

It's important to understand the concept of accounts. When you begin selling to a gallery, it will be easy enough to recognize that as an account. The same is true with a bank account. But consider that every other place where money goes or comes from—rent, utilities, transportation, materials, payroll—is also an account. The general ledger is a record of transactions made on each account. Consider them as separate entities, distinct from each other.

The most common way of keeping track of accounts is the double entry method of debits and credits. The single entry method can be used also, but double entry allows for the checks and balances necessary to reduce error. Most accounts will have two columns, one for debits (the left-hand column) and one for credits (the right-hand column). The difference between a debit and a credit is easier to understand when you consider an account as an individual apart from you. In every transaction, one person gives, another person receives. So, too, with accounts.

Say you have an account with Rainbow Gallery, which is listed in your books under accounts receivable. On Tuesday you get a check for $50 from Rainbow Gallery. The account *gives* $50 in exchange for goods, and the transaction goes into the books as a credit. (At the same time, Rainbow Gallery has an account with *your* name on it under accounts payable, which *gets* $50 worth of goods, and the transaction is listed in its own books as a debit.)

Rainbow Gallery has given $50 for goods. But how do you record the rest of the transaction? Within an account called Sales. Sales *receives* the revenue from the transaction, which is recorded as a debit of $50. Eventually Sales will give the money to an account called Bank. Sales then has a credit, and Bank is debited.

On Wednesday you receive and pay a bill for $200 from

Acme Supply, which is in your books under accounts payable. Because the account Acme Supply has received materials with a value of $200, the account is debited for that amount. You then write a check to complete the transaction. Bank gives $200 to Acme Supply (the company, not the account) and Bank is credited.

Cash and Accrual

The above examples all deal with credit. That is, goods are received before they are paid for. If cash were immediately exchanged for the goods, the entries would go into columns other than accounts payable and receivable. In bookkeeping, credit sales and purchases can be handled in one of two ways. In the cash method the transaction is recorded *when it is paid*. The accrual method records the transaction *when it is made*. In the end both yield the same results, but treating all transactions as cash transactions is easier and less confusing. Once you've adopted one method or the other, stick with it until you are forced to change (the IRS expects consistency of method over the years on your tax returns, and you must get permission from the agency to change).

Though the cash method is easier, the accrual method gives a more accurate picture of annual income, something the IRS is deeply interested in. Here's the difference. First, the cash method. It's approaching the end of your fiscal year. You have $1,000 worth of invoices to send to clients and $1,000 in bills to pay. You can minimize your income by $1,000 if you delay sending the invoices until the following year. But you can maximize your expenses by paying your bills before the end of the year.

The accrual method does not allow for such manipulation, and *the IRS requires its use if your business produces and sells merchandise and has an inventory*—which certainly applies to the crafts business. If you've shipped goods before the end of the year but have not yet been paid for them, what you *expect* to be paid is considered income for that year. If you've received materials but do not intend to pay the bills until the following year, they are still considered expenses for the current year.

Year-end inventory plays heavily in the accrual method. Products on the shelf, sold or unsold, including items on consignment, are considered as capital and must be claimed as inventory. That's why so many firms scramble to have year-end inventory close-out sales. If nothing else, it reduces the time and energy necessary for an accurate accounting of inventory. The IRS has a number of regulations regarding inventories and which method of accounting can be used. An accountant is of great help in sorting through them.

The Checking Account

The checkbook is such a common fixture in our lives that we seldom think of it as a bookkeeping tool. Yet for a business the checking account is essential. It is a means of handling and keeping track of cash transactions without the bother and risk of handling the cash itself.

With the increased use of bank debit cards, telephone banking, and computerized bill-paying programs, the use of paper checks has declined. But as a means of transferring funds from one party to another, the paper check isn't likely to disappear for a long, long time.

An accountant will rely on information in the checkbook to verify entries in other books. If you use an accounting program to record your checking-account activity, the transactions will, of course, automatically be transcribed to their related accounts.

The checking account performs another important function for your business. It's a means of keeping separate your business and personal lives. When you work for someone else it's a simple matter. All money you bring in is personal income. When you work for yourself all income still is personal, but the IRS likes to make a distinction between business and nonbusiness use of your money. This is easiest done with two checking accounts, one for business and one for nonbusiness transactions.

Technically, when you work for yourself, you neither make wages nor earn a salary. When you pay yourself, that is, take money from the business for personal use, you actually take what is called a *draw*; the draw is recorded as such in the books as a debit (the account Drawings gets the money from Bank).

Money spent on business expenses can be listed as a deduction on your tax return; drawings can't because they are personal and not business related. If you must pay business expenses out of personal funds, do not write a check on your personal account. Instead, redeposit the money into your business account, record the transaction in your cash receipts journal, and credit the Drawings account in the general ledger.

Employees

When you hire one or more employees, another complete set of bookkeeping chores becomes part of the regimen. You are responsible for withholding federal and state income taxes, social security (FICA) taxes, and workers' compensation and unemployment insurance premiums. All of these withholdings must be remitted regularly to the proper agency. Social security and workers' compensation require equal contributions by the employer and the employee. In other words, the employee pays half of the obligation, you pay the other half.

Wages paid to your spouse or children are deductible expenses. You must, however, follow the same procedures as you would with hired employees, including issuing W-2 forms and withholding taxes. Children under age 18 are exempt from social security and Medicare taxes, and they are exempt from federal and state income taxes if they are eligible to claim exempt status on Form W-4. A word of caution applies. Wages paid to family members to be used as a deduction must be physically paid and preferably kept apart from your personal account. For example, a check drawn on your business account and given to your spouse as deductible wages may not be deposited directly into your joint checking account. As you can see, if this were allowed, every business in America would break even by April 15.

If you plan to hire employees, you will need to file Form SS-4 to acquire an employer ID number. For more specific information on withholdings and state and federal regulations regarding employees, or to obtain tax tables and remittance forms, contact both the IRS and your state's revenue department.

Petty Cash

A petty cash fund is an easy way to take care of day-to-day nickel-and-dime expenses that come up in all businesses. A petty cash fund is easy to maintain provided all receipts are accounted for and only one person is in charge of the fund. To start a petty cash fund, simply withdraw a fixed amount of money, say $50, from the bank and place the cash in a box or an envelope. When you need to make a cash purchase, the cash is readily available. The important thing to remember is when you remove money, you must replace it with a receipt for the goods or services bought (and don't forget to return the change to the fund). This way the fund always balances; there always is $50 in *value* within the fund represented by cash and receipts. When the fund gets low on cash, tally the receipts and write another check for the exact amount to refurbish the fund. Record the transactions, then store the receipts.

Invoicing and Following Up

When you ship merchandise on credit, always include an invoice instead of sending it later. Technically, payment is due upon receipt of goods, but it's common practice for people not to even consider payment until they have an invoice in hand. An invoice contains the same information as the order: names and addresses, terms, shipping data, damage claim conditions and limitations, quantity and description of merchandise and their prices, and the grand total. The invoice should also include a serial number for reference. The difference between the invoice and the packing list is that the invoice is a bill. It is official notification that you wish to be paid under the agreed-upon terms.

File a duplicate copy of the invoice in an accounts receivable file until it is paid. In a perfect world you receive your money within thirty to forty-five days.

In a less than perfect world you have to ask again to be paid. Each month review your accounts receivable file to see which accounts are overdue. Move these accounts into another file for closer scrutiny and promptly resubmit a bill. Some standard invoice forms come with several copies, with subsequent copies preprinted with polite reminders. If you don't use this kind of form, make a photocopy of the invoice or write up a new bill with a courteous reminder. If you haven't received payment within fifteen days of a second billing, once again resubmit, this time with a slightly sterner reminder. How long you wish to continue billing is up to you, but keep in mind the longer a bill goes unpaid, the more difficult it is to collect. If an account is more than sixty days past due, consider turning it over to a collection agency. An agency charges you a percentage, but you at least get something for your effort. Do not, however, contact an agency without first warning the account of your intentions. First, it is the ethical thing to do; second, it often inspires prompt payment.

All businesses are different for the simple reason that all businesses are run by different people. True, all businesses must adhere to certain minimum standards as far as operation and record keeping, but what happens after that is entirely up to the operators of the business. As far as bookkeeping is concerned, the simplest system that covers all the bases is all that is necessary. Which bases need to be covered is dependent on the size and complexity of the business. The most important thing to remember about keeping track of money is to carefully record where it comes from and where it goes.

Keeping records is a tedious, time-consuming process that requires dedication to make it work effectively. IRS considerations aside, adequate record keeping tells you many things about the state of your business. It gives you an ongoing picture of where you stand as far as income and expenses. Better to know about problems as they arise than have a year-end surprise. And because you are constantly aware of your financial standing, you can take steps to minimize problems. Sales mean nothing if they are not ahead of expenses. No business can operate at a loss for long. If you don't know where the money goes—and how much of it is going—you have no idea where costs can be cut.

The Taxman and You

"In this world nothing is certain but death and taxes." Benjamin Franklin said that, and once said, it was inevitable that the Internal Revenue Service would prove him right. After all, who would be bold enough to put the lie to Franklin?

Indeed, taxes are so much a part of life that many business decisions are based solely on the resulting tax implications. Regardless of what you think of Uncle Sam's taxing powers, all of us must annually share with the government certain information to establish our tax liabilities. If we do not owe taxes, we must show why in that sheaf of paperwork known as the return.

The tax system is set up in such a way that profit-seeking businesses are taxed on gains rather than total income. Built into the system are ways by which taxpayers can offset or reduce overall gain and reduce their tax liability. Sometimes these are called *deductions*. Other times they are called *loopholes*. The goal of the IRS is to collect as much in taxes as it can. The goal of the taxpayer is to take advantage of as many (legal) deductions as possible to pay as little tax as possible. The IRS makes a habit of reviewing tax returns to see whether taxpayers are playing by the rules. In general, the IRS will not point out deductions you could have taken, but it will inform you of deductions you shouldn't have taken. Sometimes this is deemed an honest mistake. In more serious cases it is called *fraud*.

The IRS allows you to deduct reasonable business-related expenses to offset your income from that business. It even allows you to use a business loss to offset gains from another source. A loss is when you spend more money on your business than the business brings in. For self-employed people, profit or loss shows up on Schedule C *(Profit or Loss from Business or Profession)* and is reported on Line 12 of Form 1040.

Note: References to specific line numbers, forms, and schedules are based on 1994 returns. The information provided in this section is general and should not be taken as tax advice. Bear in mind also that tax laws are always changing from one year to the next. What's more, as of this writing, major changes in the tax code may be expected as a result of the recent shift to Republican party control in both the Senate and the House of Representatives.

Home Sweet Studio

Working at home is one of the delightful aspects of being self-employed. There's no commute, it's convenient, you can work when you please, and you don't have to face the world on those days when you don't—or the world doesn't—look so rosy. What's more, it's a good way to keep costs down. And there are a handful of tax deductions you can take that otherwise would be unavailable.

The IRS, however, has a stringent set of rules that craftspersons, or anyone operating a business from the home, must follow. In other words, your home must qualify for the deductions. Foremost, the portion of your home, or outbuilding on your property, used for business must be used exclusively for business and on a regular basis. Second, your home studio or shop must be your principal place of business.

If each day after breakfast you spread out your crafts work on the dining room table, the IRS will disallow the deduction. Only if the dining room is set aside for exclusive business use will it qualify. It qualifies, that is, if you use it on a regular basis. What constitutes a "regular basis" is open to interpretation. There is no set minimum number of hours or days magically separating regular from irregular. But if you are serious about earning money by your craft, then meeting this requirement is easy enough. The idea is to avoid occasional or nonessential use.

The stipulation that your home be your principal place of

business should not be much of a problem. Because of the nature of the crafts business, either you work at home or you don't. Admittedly there may be some exceptions. If you have a shop in town and sometimes bring work home as a matter of convenience, work you could just as easily do at the shop, any deductions you take would be open to question. This rule applies more to a professional—an attorney for example— who has an office away from home but reads legal briefs and law books in his den each evening. No home-use deductions would be allowed in this case.

Your crafts business need not be your sole source of income for your home to qualify as your principal place of business. You can have another job and operate your crafts business at home and still qualify. Principal place of business refers to the business in question.

Assuming your home qualifies, figure your deductions the same way you determined home-business-use costs in previous analyses. Determine what percentage of space you use for your business and multiply that by the overall costs that apply. You can deduct allocable portions of mortgage interest, property taxes, rent, utilities, depreciation, and repair and maintenance. A word of caution: If you deduct the allocable portions of mortgage interest and property taxes on Schedule C, you may only deduct the remaining portions on Schedule A *(Itemized Deductions)*. You may fully deduct expenses that are exclusive to your workplace. In all cases the deductions must be "reasonable."

Expenses for office use of the home are figured on Form 8829 and transferred to Schedule C, Line 30.

The IRS will not allow you to use home-use deductions to create or increase a loss and thereby reduce taxable income from other sources. Those deductions are limited to your net income and cannot cause the net income to drop below zero. First you must reduce your gross income by expenses *excluding* those for your home studio. Only then can you begin deducting expenses for your home studio and in the following order: interest and taxes, operating expenses, and depreciation. If and when you reach zero, you must stop. You can, however, carry over unused deductions to the next year. One more point: Because you can fully itemize mortgage interest and property taxes on Schedule A, you needn't bother with them on Schedule C unless it's more advantageous to do so. An accountant can give you the best advice on this matter.

The Hobby Loss Limitation Rule

The IRS is skeptical of people who year after year claim losses from a business that is supposed to be profitable. The taxman begins to wonder whether such people are truly engaged in business with the intent of making a profit, or if they are merely engaged in a hobby, which may be fun but is no more a business than taking a hike.

Nearly all income, including income from a hobby, is taxable. The IRS has nothing against hobbies even if they earn money, so it allows you to negate that income with expenses incurred in pursuit of your hobby. But to ensure that hobbyists don't take undue advantage of business deductions, the IRS established the hobby loss limitation rule. The IRS will not allow you to take a loss on your hobby. In other words, you may deduct hobby expenses only up to the amount of your hobby income.

What's more, if you are a hobbyist (or a businessperson deemed by the IRS to be a hobbyist), you may not use Schedule C. Income from a hobby is reported on Form 1040, Line 21, as "other income." Your personal deductions are claimed on Schedule A, Line 20, "miscellaneous deductions."

But there is a catch. In order for hobby expenses to be eligible for the write-off, your *total* miscellaneous deductions must be more than two percent of your adjusted gross income (Form 1040, Line 31).

Naturally, by now you are asking, perhaps indignantly, "What's all this have to do with me? I'm not a hobbyist, I'm a businessperson. I have a legitimate crafts business." All good points. And if you've turned a profit during three of the last five years, the above discussion on hobbies may have little or nothing to do with you. But it could have more to do with you than you think.

The IRS is interested in your intention of making a profit. It presumes that if you are in business, profit is your intention, not garnering write-offs to offset other income. The IRS has established two tests to help determine whether that venture is a hobby or a business. One of these is the objective "three years out of five" test. If you, as the sole proprietor of a crafts business, realized a profit in three of the last five years, then there is at least the presumption of intent to make a profit. (Before the Tax Reform Act of 1986, one needed to show a profit in two out of five years.) If you pass this test and the IRS still questions your intent to make a profit, it is up to the IRS to prove a lack of intent.

If you fail the test, you have two choices. You can amend previous years' returns to reflect profits rather than losses (and pay any taxes and penalties owed). Or you can attempt to prove intent to make a profit by the subjective second test of "facts and circumstances."

The IRS has established nine determining factors against which your profit intent is measured. All nine factors listed below are considered together, and no one of them is conclusive.

1. Do you carry out the affairs of your business in a businesslike manner? Do you make use of generally accepted accounting methods? Do you have written contracts with clients?

2. What expertise and training do you have? Do you have any credentials? Have you won any awards for your work? Do you read books and trade journals related to your craft and to the crafts trade in general? Do you consult regularly with an accountant or an attorney about your business?

3. How much time and effort do you put into your business? Do you work on it in your spare time away from another income-producing activity, or did you forsake another activity to pursue your crafts business?

4. How much of an investment have you made in the assets of your business, and do you expect those assets to

appreciate in value? Once you've gained recognition in your field, do you believe the value of your crafts will increase because of your reputation?

5. Have you been successful in other business ventures?

6. What is the history of receipts and losses of your business? Even though you've failed to make a profit, are receipts increasing and costs decreasing? If not, can you explain increasing losses?

7. What is the relationship between profitable years and years in which you incurred a loss? Can you explain why you had a large loss following a profitable year? If your receipts or profits are merely occasional, how substantial are they as compared with your investment in the business? Small returns for a large investment may indicate a lack of profit motive.

8. What is your financial status? Do you rely on your business income as a necessary supplement to other income, or do you use your business to generate tax benefits for an adequate income from another source?

9. What are your personal motives for carrying out your business activities? Do they deal more with pleasurable or recreational elements rather than with profit motive?

As a craftsperson, you might have a tough time swallowing the last question. Of course you take pleasure in your work; that's why you do it. Taking pleasure in your work does not preclude profit motive. But can you demonstrate you are not in business (and taking losses) just for the fun of it?

If, while trying to establish a profitable crafts business, you have incurred losses over several years, your ability to demonstrate intent will figure largely if you are audited.

Between Form 1040 and a Hard Place

The Tax Reform Act of 1986 was passed by Congress to simplify the tax structure and make it more equitable. A portion of that act, the uniform capitalization rules, has proved to be one of the most contentious among craftspersons and others involved in creative endeavors. The rules apply to year-end inventory.

Businesses that maintain inventories always have had to account for them on their tax returns. Unsold crafts (including crafts held on consignment by others), raw materials, and work in progress have a value and therefore must be included as capital assets. This is nothing new. Craftspersons merely determined the worth of their inventory based on costs, not actual price, and noted the figure on the proper line (Schedule C, Part I, Line 4, "cost of goods sold").

In the past, certain direct and indirect costs, called *period costs*, were fully deductible during the year incurred. The new capitalization rules changed all that by mandating that more costs must be included in inventory than before. That is, certain expenditures are treated as assets and are included as inventory, not as expenses. The result is that period costs that were once fully deductible in the year incurred must now be apportioned to each item in the inventory and amortized; deductions cannot be taken until the year the item is sold.

For example: You are a leather worker who in 1985 bought a new set of tools for $100. You deducted the full cost of the tools as a legitimate business expense. The cost of the tools was not included in your pricing calculations and, therefore, did not figure into your inventory at year's end. Now assume you purchased the tools in 1987, the first year the new capitalization rules went into effect. In that year, with those tools, you made one hundred belts valued at $10 each, not including the cost of the tools. But you sold only sixty belts that year. The new rules state that you must apportion the value of the tools to each item produced by them, and that you may take a deduction for the tools only for those items sold, or $60. Since you have forty belts left in your inventory, each belt is valued at $11 instead of $10. Further deductions for the tools can be taken only when the individual belts are sold, or entirely after two years even if the belts are not sold.

The matter of the cost of one set of tools applied to a single item is relatively easy to follow and keep an accounting of. But the new rules apply to all costs casually related to production. When you consider that a portion of utilities costs, warehousing costs, general administrative costs, depreciation, and dozens of other costs must be allocated to each item in inventory and amortized, an accounting nightmare becomes a daily reality.

Now for the *good* bad news. Craftspersons can elect to use IRS Resolution 88-62, promulgated in 1988. Also called the *safe harbor*, it states that you can deduct 50 percent of the expenses in the year they were incurred and 25 percent in each of the two successive years. If you have no inventory at the end of the year, that is, no goods to which costs can be attributed, your costs incurred during the year are fully deductible.

You can't be involved in the crafts community for long without hearing or reading about the debate over the difference between art and craft. It's been going on for years and years and likely will go on for years and years to come. But as far as the IRS is concerned the case is closed. At least for now.

The new rule applies chiefly to manufacturers, contractors, wholesalers, and retailers—all firms with inventories. "Manufacturer" is an exceedingly broad category, one that encompasses anyone who produces "tangible personal property," according to the IRS. Initially this included artists, craftspersons, photographers, writers, and all manner of creative people who produced goods for sale. But the hue and cry was loud and long. Artists for Tax Equity and the Writers Coalition, among others, lobbied Congress ardently for exemptions, claiming that the rules placed excessive and unmanageable burdens on members of the art community.

Unfortunately, the voice from the crafts community came too softly and too late. In late 1988, Congress passed a law exempting from the uniform capitalization rules artists "whose personal efforts create or may reasonably be expected to create a literary manuscript, musical composition, dance score, photograph, photographic negative or transparency, picture, painting, sculpture, statue, etching, drawing, cartoon, graphic design, or original print edition." People thus referred to could continue to deduct certain expenses as they always had, in the year in which they occurred.

There was some argument on behalf of craftspersons, but Congress insisted that they are still manufacturers of tangible goods. But aren't artists and writers? Perhaps yes, perhaps no. It depends on which side of the art versus craft fence you stand. As far as Congress is concerned—at least as it applies to the tax code—the fence is composed of solid blocks of utility. If the work produced is remotely utilitarian, then it is subject to the capitalization rules. What is utilitarian and what is not is open to debate, but "jewelry, silverware, pottery, furniture, and other similar household items" were expressly excluded from exemption.

On Crafts and Craftsmanship

PEOPLE HAVE ALWAYS been drawn to things made by hand. In the past, it was the only way things were made. If you needed a bowl or pouch in which to gather berries, you made one. If you needed a weapon for hunting or defense, you made one. As time passed, some individuals became better than others at making certain things. The family or clan or tribe or village came to depend on these better-skilled persons for the goods they found useful and, eventually, necessary. The craftsperson came into his own. With practice came skill and knowledge, which was passed from generation to generation. With skill and knowledge came refinements that increased the apparent value of some items. A knife, for example, was no longer necessarily just a tool for cutting, but it could be a thing of beauty as well. As a thing of beauty it had aesthetic value. With aesthetic value came pride of ownership.

Not everyone, however, could own an aesthetically pleasing object, no matter how utilitarian. Social status determined who could own what. The higher the status the greater the demand and ability to pay for finer things. There emerged a distinction between things of purely utilitarian and aesthetic value. But just as status determined who could own things of "quality," it also determined the caste of those who made them. Craftspersons were workers, crafts a humble occupation. In fact potters were once among the lowest of the low. The only true forms of art were painting and sculpture.

With the Industrial Revolution, society had less and less need for handcrafted utilitarian goods. A plentiful supply of necessities could now be made one after another by machines and a slew of production workers. Aesthetic value was compromised. No matter. The masses had little need or use for aesthetics. Historically, the less leisure time a given group had, the less interest it had in aesthetics: Energy was better spent on survival.

But there always have been those who could afford the work of craftspersons and artists and had the leisure to enjoy it. And when the nature of crafts transformed from a primarily utilitarian function to one of aesthetic function, buyers of crafts became not *consumers* but *patrons*.

In older days, craftspersons belonged to guilds, which were the academies of craft. Knowledge and skills were closely guarded secrets for the protection of the members of the various trades and of the integrity of the various crafts.

Today, guilds no longer play the role they once did. And more and more of the masses, now that their energies are not directed solely toward survival, have the ability to buy and enjoy things of quality and beauty.

Pride of owning unique and aesthetically pleasing things made by hand is a powerful motivator. Beautiful things enhance the environment and help stimulate the well-being of the inhabitants. And few can deny the status involved in owning valuable works of art and craft.

Though guilds have lost their power and function, craftspersons have not. The contemporary craftsperson has an unstated obligation, mandated by centuries of tradition, to protect the integrity of his individual craft, and crafts in general, and to pass his knowledge on to capable hands for the continued enjoyment of all.

With all the emphasis on business and professionalism, the inescapable fact is that crafts is foremost a culture, lifestyle, and legacy.

WHOLESALE CRAFTS
TRADE-SHOW
PROMOTERS

AMC Trade Shows
1933 S. Broadway
Suite 111
Los Angeles, CA 90007
213 747-3488

American Craft Enterprises, Inc.
21 S. Etlings Corner Rd.
Highland, NY 12528
800 836-3470

Americana Sampler, Inc.
P.O. Box 160009
Nashville, TN 37216
615 227-2084

Heritage Markets
P.O. Box 389
Carlisle, PA 17013
717 249-9404
717 258-0265 fax

George Little Management Co.
10 Bank St.
Suite 1200
White Plains, NY 10606-1933
800 272-SHOW
914 948-6194 fax

Industry Productions of America
P.O. Box 27337
Los Angeles, CA 90027
213 962-5424
213 962-6040 fax

LA Mart (California Gift Show)
1933 S. Broadway
Los Angeles, CA 90007
800 LAMART4
213 749-7911

Merchandise Mart Properties
Suite 470
The Merchandise Mart
200 World Trade Center
Chicago, IL 60654-9963
800 677-6278
312 527-7782 fax

The Rosen Group
Suite 300 Mill Centre
3000 Chestnut Ave.
Baltimore, MD 21211
410 889-2933
410 889-1320 fax

Roy Helms and Associates
1142 Auahi St.
Suite 2820
Honolulu, HI 96814
808 422-7362
808 423-1688 fax

CALENDAR OF WHOLESALE CRAFTS TRADE SHOWS

(based on 1994–95 schedule)

JANUARY

San Francisco International Gift
    Fair
George Little Management
Moscone Convention Center

New York International Gift Fair
George Little Management
Jacob Javits Convention Center

American & International Crafts—
    West
George Little Management
Moscone Convention Center,
San Francisco

Washington Gift Show
George Little Management
Washington Convention Center,
    Washington, DC

Cash & Carry Wholesale Market
Heritage Markets
Location TBA

Chicago Gifts & Accessories
    Market
Merchandise Mart Properties
The Merchandise Mart

Beckman's Hand Crafted Gift
    Show
Industry Productions of America
McCormick Place North, Chicago

Chicago Gift Show
George Little Management
McCormick Place North

Handmade in the USA
George Little Management
Passenger Ship Terminal, Pier 90,
    New York

FEBRUARY

ACC Craft Fair Baltimore
American Craft Enterprises
Baltimore Convention Center

Philadelphia Spring Buyers Market
The Rosen Group
Pennsylvania Convention Center

Heritage Market of American
    Crafts
Heritage Productions
Hilton Hotel, King of Prussia, PA

MARCH

Boston Gift Show
George Little Management
Bayside Exposition Center

San Francisco Contemporary Crafts
    Market
Roy Helms and Associates
Fort Mason Center

Beckman's Craft Supplier
Industry Productions of America
Long Beach Convention Center,
    Los Angeles

APRIL

ACC Craft Fair St. Paul
American Craft Enterprises
St. Paul Civic Center

New York Table Top Show
George Little Management
26th St. Armory

MAY

Boston Buyers Market
The Rosen Agency
Bayside Exposition Center

International Contemporary
    Furniture Fair
George Little Management
Jacob Javits Convention Center,
    New York

Santa Monica Contemporary Crafts
    Market
Roy Helms and Associates
Santa Monica Civic Center

JUNE

ACC Craft Fair Columbus
American Craft Enterprises
Columbus Convention Center,
    Columbus, OH

Kansas City Country Market
Americana Sampler
Kansas City Merchandise Mart,
    Overland Park, KS

Cash & Carry Wholesale Market
Heritage Market of American
    Crafts
King of Prussia, PA

Fort Washington Summer Market
Americana Sampler
Fort Washington Expo Center, PA

JULY

Boston Buyers Market
The Rosen Group
Expo Center

Beckman's Gift Show
Industry Productions of America
Los Angeles Sports Arena

Beckman's Handcrafted Gift Show
Industry Productions of America
ExpoCenter, Chicago

California Gift Show
AMC Trade Shows
Los Angeles Convention Center

Chicago Gift Show
George Little Management Co.
McCormick Place North and Expo
    Center

Cash & Carry Wholesale Markets
Heritage Market of American
    Crafts
Kane County Fairgrounds, St.
    Charles, IL

Washington Gift Show
George Little Management
Washington Convention Center,
    Washington, DC

AUGUST

San Francisco International Gift
    Fair
George Little Management
Moscone Convention Center

ACC Craft Fair San Francisco
American Craft Enterprises
Fort Mason Center

New York International Gift Fair
George Little Management
Jacob Javits Convention Center

SEPTEMBER

Los Angeles Fall Gift & Jewelry
   Mart
AMC Trade Shows
LA Convention Center

LA Mart Fall Gift & Decorative
   Accessories Market
LAM
LA Mart

Boston Gift Show
George Little Management
Bayside Exposition Center

OCTOBER

Phoenix Gift & Jewelry Show
AMC Trade Shows
Phoenix Civic Plaza

New York Home Textiles Show
George Little Management
Jacob Javits Convention Center

New York Table Top Show
George Little Management
26th St. Armory

PUBLICATIONS

The ArtFair SourceBook
1234 South Dixie Hwy. #111
Coral Gables, FL 33146
800 358-2045

   $95 for initial edition, $50 for yearly renewal. A resource book of more than 250 craft events, including locations, phone numbers, fees, deadlines, and more.

The Crafts Fair Guide (quarterly)
P.O. Box 5508
Mill Valley, CA 94942
415 332-7687

   $42.50 per year. Specific to California retail fairs. Features dates, locations, fees, deadlines, reviews, and ratings.

The Crafts Report (monthly)
P.O. Box 1992
Wilmington, DE 19899
302 656-2209
800 777-7098
302 656-4894 fax

   $25.95 per year. Features a wide range of up-to-date information of interest to professional craftspersons, wholesale and retail fair calendars, reviews, news.

Craft Supply Magazine (quarterly)
225 Gordon's Corner Plaza
Box 420
Manalapan, NJ 07726
908 446-4900
908 446-5488 fax

   $30 per year. Subscribers receive annual directory

BIBLIOGRAPHY

Bealer, Alex. *The Successful Craftsman: Making Your Craft Your Business.* Barre, Mass.: Barre Publishing, 1975.

Brabec, Barbara. *Creative Crafts: How to Sell Your Crafts, Needlework, Designs & Know-how.* Barrington, Ill.: Countryside Books, 1979.

Clark, Douglas L. *Starting a Successful Business on the West Coast.* Vancouver, B.C., Canada: Self-Counsel Press, 1982.

Clark, Leta. *How to Make Money with Your Crafts.* New York: Morrow, 1973.

Cornish, Clive G. *Basic Accounting for the Small Business.* Vancouver, B.C., Canada: Self-Counsel Press, 1977.

Dowd, Merle E. *How to Earn More Money from Your Crafts.* Garden City, N.Y.: Doubleday, 1976.

DuBoff, Leonard D. *The Law (in Plain English) for Craftspeople.* Seattle: Madrona Publishers, 1984.

Emmert, Philip, and William C. Donaghy. *Human Communication: Elements and Contexts.* New York: Random House, 1981.

H & R Block. *1995 Income Tax Guide.* New York: Simon & Schuster, 1994.

Maxwell, David. *The Exhibit Medium: Theory and Practice of Trade Show Participation.* New York: Successful Meetings Magazine, 1978.

The Price Waterhouse Guide to the New Tax Law. New York: Bantam, 1986.

The Price Waterhouse Personal Tax Advisor. New York: Bantam, 1987.

Scott, Michael. *The Crafts Business Encyclopedia: Marketing, Management and Money.* New York: Harcourt Brace Jovanovich, 1979.

Stanton, William J. *Fundamentals of Marketing.* New York: McGraw Hill, 1964.

Wettlaufer, George and Nancy. *The Craftsman's Survival Manual.* Englewood Cliffs, N.J.: Prentice-Hall, 1974.

Wingate, John W., and Harland E. Samson. *Retail Merchandising.* Cincinnati: South-Western, 1968.

Whitaker, Irwin. *Crafts and Craftsmen.* Dubuque, Iowa: Wm. C. Brown, 1967.